DELICIOUS WHOLE NECTAR®

POWER Smoothies

Bob & Wendy Mulligan

Delicious Whole Nectar
Power Smoothies

ISBN 0-9727926-0-0

Published by Whole Nectar Press
Denver, Colorado

These Are Not Just
Any Smoothie Recipes!

Smoothies are everywhere. Almost any and every fruity drink is called a smoothie. For the most part, typical commercial smoothies are various combinations of ice cream, frozen yogurt, fruit syrup and artificial flavorings. Some are just fruit juice and a little yogurt in a bottle. Other smoothies are like glorified sno cones - a lot of fruit syrup and ice. Sometimes a microscopic amount of real fruit is added to the mixture. Most are high calorie and nutritionally pretty weak.

That's not the kind of smoothie you'll find in this book. Anybody can put ice cream in a blender and come up with something that tastes good. The real accomplishment is a blend that has both great flavor and superior nutrition. That's what Whole Nectar Power Smoothies are all about - vibrant flavor and power packed nutrition.

We're very proud of our lively smoothie menu. Many of them are stimulating blends of fresh fruit flavors. Our Power Smoothie collection includes everything from All-American, traditional smoothies like *Just Peach*, to more exotic blends like *Jamaican Mango Tangerine*. You'll find comforting smoothies like *Vanilla Blueberry Banana* and adventurous ones like *Strawberry Daiquiri*.

But, our collection of recipes doesn't stop there. Our *Power Coffee Shake* and *Chai Apple Smoothie* are guaranteed to energize. Or, how about a *Power Frostee* or *Vanilla Super Malt*? And, if you're one of the many fans of soymilk, we'll show you an easy way to make your own super soymilk.

Even though our smoothies have a wide variety of flavors, they all have a couple of things in common. First - All of our blends have a balance of healthy protein from our own Whole Nectar Ultimate Soy Protein Smoothie Mix. Whether you're whirling a *Kiwi Pineapple Smoothie* or a *Cinnamon Peanut Butter Smoothie*, the mild flavor of our Ultimate Soy Protein Smoothie Mix is the perfect protein base. Second - All of our recipes are specifically written for the Vita-Mix® machine. As professional smoothie mixologists, we know it's the only blender that can process whole fruits and lots of ice into velvety smooth, gourmet quality power drinks.

Nobody has put the time and effort into Smoothie R&D the way we have. We've done all the legwork to pull together a turnkey system for making healthy and delicious smoothies. Besides this book, all you need is Whole Nectar Ultimate Soy Protein Smoothie Mix, your favorite flavors and a Vita-Mix® machine. It's the easy way to do something good for yourself.

Smoothie R&D

Are you trying to eat a little better? Do you feel torn between the imperative to eat right and no time to do it? Are you riddled with guilt every time you see a magazine article with yet another reminder that your fruit and vegetable eating habits aren't what they should be? Well, you're not alone. We used to be in the same boat. Then a breakthrough. The secret to the breakthrough? Our blender. Over time we discovered that our blender was responsible for all but eliminating our struggle to eat more fruits and vegetables - more whole grains - more whole foods of all kinds.

This discovery inspired us to look for a way to show other people how to blend good health and great taste in a glass. We discovered the Vita-Mix® Company and before we knew it we were on the road demonstrating their blender as a healthy eating tool. We had used several different name brand blenders over the years, but we found the Vita-Mix® to be something else altogether. While demonstrating this amazing machine for many thousands of people all over the country, we were in the perfect position to begin some serious Smoothie R&D. We began perfecting a collection of smoothie recipes that were both tasty and healthy. In addition to recipe testing, all those hours behind the blender produced a wealth of blender related tips, shortcuts and just plain old good ideas. Much of what we learned from our "test kitchen on the road" became the basis of this book.

But we didn't stop there.

The Science Of Power Smoothie Mixology

We kept whirling right along, staying in touch with the latest solid health information. When soy began to get some impressive health press, we thought it would be a good idea to add some soy protein powder to the smoothies we were already making. We bought some at a local health food store and were pretty disappointed with the taste. Then we tried another soy protein powder and another until we had literally blended up everything on the market. None of them really tasted very good and the ones that tasted a little better were loaded with sugar. Thinking we were missing something, we trotted around to quite a few commercial smoothie establishments. There we found smoothies that tasted good (how could you miss with whirled ice cream or fruit syrup) but from a nutritional standpoint we were obliged to give them failing grades. Somewhere between calorie-laden ice cream concoctions and mixtures reminiscent of blended lawn clippings, we realized we had discovered a black hole in the science of smoothie mixology. The great tasting, healthy, protein powered smoothie did not exist.

But we didn't see any reason it couldn't exist. That idea propelled us to explore the next level of smoothie science. The X factor appeared to be the protein source. To qualify as a mini-meal or substantial snack we wanted our smoothies to have a healthy balance of protein. Based on the growing body of health evidence, soy was the protein source we wanted to use. In addition, we knew the real health benefits were from soy foods made from whole soybeans. All the soy protein powders we saw didn't use the whole soybean. They used just the protein part of the bean (called soy isolate) and discarded the rest.

So we started from scratch and found premium sweet soybeans that required very little sweetening. The next step was locating a processing method that produced a formula with a mild, nutty flavor - complete with the nutrition of whole soybeans. With a boost of additional protein and calcium, we knew we had the formula we wanted.

Aside from the fact that our formula has the nutrition of whole soy foods, what people like most about our Ultimate Soy Protein Smoothie Mix is the mild, almost neutral taste of the mix. That characteristic, plus the fact that our mix is only minimally sweetened, makes it the perfect protein base for any flavor of smoothie. The flavor and sweetness in Whole Nectar Smoothies comes from the fresh fruits and other foods blended with the smoothie mix, not from complicated artificial flavorings within our mix. For example, we don't make a strawberry flavored smoothie mix because there's no way artificial strawberry flavoring and red dye #12 can take the place of freshly blended strawberries. And we're proud of the fact that, unlike many products on the market that have ingredient lists as long as your arm, our ingredient list is short and comes essentially from real foods - not from a laboratory.

Our Whole Nectar Ultimate Soy Protein Smoothie Mix has now been on the market for several years. It continues to be a one-of-a-kind product with a growing fan club.

It's A Balance

As important as protein is to power smoothies, there's more to it than that. The perfect smoothie is a balance of frozen and unfrozen ingredients. That's where our recipe guide comes in handy. We've taken all the guesswork out of determining the right proportions of ingredients to make a great smoothie. Besides our Whole Nectar Ultimate Soy Protein Smoothie Mix, the other elements of the perfect power smoothie are whole foods, sweetening and ice. Here's some information about each one so that you can become a smoothie expert in your own right.

Whole Foods

There's no substitute for the full flavors of fresh, ripe fruit, real almonds or sweet dates. What a bonus! The same whole foods with deliciously distinctive flavors, colors and aromas are also good for you. But, it's the whole fruit, the whole almond and the whole date that are the key to both full flavor and maximum nutrition. A glass of apple juice, for instance, can't compete with a low calorie, high fiber, nutrient dense whole apple. That's why our power smoothie recipes feature items from the produce department rather than the beverage aisle.

Many of our power smoothie recipes rely on a variety of fresh ripe fruit for flavor. We have also found that many unsweetened, frozen fruits (particularly berries and peaches) are tasty, handy to have on hand, and just as nutritious as fresh according to people who know these things.

Wash all fruits and vegetables thoroughly and peel and /or seed according to the directions. Many fruit seeds are very nutritious but not all of them taste good. If the directions tell you to leave out the seeds or use seedless varieties (like grapes) it's probably because the strong flavor in the seeds would ruin the taste of the smoothie. Many fruits and vegetables don't have to be peeled. In fact, in many cases, it's healthier not to peel them. In addition, don't discard nutritional gold mines like the core of the pineapple or the white pith of citrus fruit. The Vita-Mix® will easily process these fibrous parts of the fruit and blend it into your smoothie using "stealth technology". See our *To Peel Or Not To Peel* chart in the back of the book for tips on what to keep and what to discard.

If you have a Vita-Mix® machine there's no need to pre-chop fruit or thaw out frozen ingredients. The machine will easily smooth out these ingredients.

Sweetener

All of our smoothie recipes aim for a medium level of sweetness. In many cases ripe, fresh fruit or fruit frozen at the height of ripeness along with the mild sweetness of our smoothie mix is all that's needed. When you want more, juice concentrates are a great way to punch up the flavor and sweetness that's diluted by ice. Look for juice concentrates that are all fruit rather than corn syrup and artificial flavoring. Orange, peach, apple, grape and raspberry flavors are good ones to have handy in your freezer. We typically keep the juice concentrates frozen and just spoon out the amount needed for the smoothie. But you can also let the juice concentrates thaw out in your refrigerator and pour out the amount needed.

Our other favorite sweeteners are honey, Florida Crystals (a natural milled cane sugar found in health food stores and many supermarkets) and whole, pitted dates. Certainly, any other sweetening of your choice or artificial sweetener will work in our recipes. You might need to experiment, because all sweeteners are not equal. For example, a teaspoon of honey is much sweeter than a teaspoon of sugar.

We think our smoothies have a good balance of sweetness. However, we're certain you'll want to make adjustments from time to time. The sweetness of fruit is a variable as well as personal preferences. If you're the kind of person that tends to think almost everything is too sweet, you may want to substitute water for half the juice concentrate in recipes or cut in half any added honey or sugar. On the other hand, if you'd prefer a sweeter smoothie, add small amounts of juice concentrate, honey or Florida Crystals until you've hit the mark that's right for you. Whatever experimenting you do, the proportions in our recipes are a good place to start. Then make small adjustments until you have the perfect custom blend.

Ice

The perfect smoothie is a balance of frozen and unfrozen ingredients. Ice not only chills the ingredients, but is also a thickener. Whether your blend is thin, like a milk shake, or thick enough to make a spoon stand up, is determined primarily by the amount of ice you use. Our smoothie recipes use a ratio of frozen and unfrozen ingredients designed to produce a fairly thick smoothie. The shake recipes in this book produce a blend that is not as thick and icy as the smoothies. With this principle in mind, you can modify any smoothie recipe thicker or thinner according to your preference.

Another variable is that all ice is not the same. If you have a choice, try to avoid using soft ice (grocery store bagged ice, crushed, shaved, mini-cubes etc.). In the Vita-Mix®, the best smoothies are made with hard ice from standard ice cube trays or larger shapes made by home icemakers. Why is hard ice better? You use less. Ice dilutes flavor so less ice means more flavor.

One variation on the use of frozen ingredients is the substitution of frozen fruit for most or all of the ice in a recipe. This produces a blend that's thick, almost creamy in texture, and very flavorful. The *Orange Blackberry Kiwi Smoothie* is one example of this type of smoothie. If you like the creamy texture of this smoothie, you'll find that almost any recipe can be modified to this style by using lots of frozen fruit and little or no ice.

Processing ice and frozen fruit may be the most outstanding feature of the Vita-Mix® machine. With this blender, you don't have to crush ice first or gingerly drop in ice cubes one at a time. All the smoothie ingredients, including the ice, go into the blender in one step. Thirty seconds later you have a world class smoothie. Speaking of ice - it causes the death of many blenders. But you don't have to worry about that with the Vita-Mix®. The Vita-Mix® machine in our house has had what we would call "extremely heavy use" for 8 years and it works like a champ every time.

Some Starter Tips From Our Smoothie Institute

Although we wouldn't want to be accused of trying to squelch anyone's creative juices, our experience compels us to recommend that you follow a few recipes fairly closely before you strike out on your own. And if you're a new Vita-Mix® owner, this suggestion goes double. While it's tempting to load the blender with random items and hope it tastes good, we're sure you'll be happier with the results by following some specific instructions, at least in the beginning. The machine is easy to use but the right proportions of ingredients are hard to guess without following some guidelines. Once you have a feel for these proportions, then, by all means, have fun being creative.

All of our smoothie recipes aim for a balance of healthy protein and good taste. The amount of smoothie mix we recommend in each recipe is a good guideline but certainly something you can modify for your own tastes. If you've never used soy protein powder before, you may want to start with half the amount recommended in the recipe and increase it to suit your tastes.

In many of our recipes we refer to a specific brand name product like Yoplait® and Welch's®. No, those companies haven't paid us to use their products in the book. We just like them and use them ourselves. From our time as professional demonstrators, we know that many people wanted to know exactly what we used to make a smoothie because it made grocery shopping more of a no-brainer for them. If you've ever stood there staring at 8 different kinds of orange juice, unable to make a decision, then you know what we mean. However, don't let our listing of very specific brands and flavors paralyze you into not making anything. Feel free to use any kind that's handy. It will taste great. Smoothies are better when served immediately. We don't generally recommend storing them for later use. Any recipe can be scaled up or down in size so that you have just the right amount for the occasion.

Don't miss our *Smoothie Clinic, 9 Ways Power Smoothies Can Be The Centerpiece Of A Healthy Lifestyle, How To Pick the Best Fruit* and our other sections in the back of the book. We think we have some good information there you won't want to miss.

Now get whirling and have fun.

The rich variety of healthy foods
found in today's supermarkets
and a blender in your kitchen,
open the door for some interesting
and tasty quick meals and snacks.

Power Smoothies

Contents

It's a jungle out there!

Mango, kiwi, pineapple, and guava
are just a few of the many tropical fruits
that are no longer hard-to-find
exotics in most supermarkets. Tropical
flavored smoothie combinations are
endless and never boring.

(continued)

Orange Raspberry Banana Smoothie

Citrus fruit has so many healthful qualities, it's a good idea to have some every day. Enjoying this smoothie is a great way to do just that.

1/3 cup Welch's® White Grape Raspberry frozen juice concentrate
1/4 cup water
1 scoop (5 tablespoons) **Whole Nectar® Ultimate Soy Protein Smoothie Mix**
1 orange (peeled & halved)
1 frozen banana (broken in thirds)
1-1/4 to 1-3/4 cups ice

Makes about 20 oz.

Place all ingredients in the Vita-Mix container in order listed. Secure the lid. Select Variable #1, turn to ON, and quickly increase speed to #10. Switch to HIGH. Run about 20 seconds until smooth. Use tamper, if necessary, to help circulate ingredients.

251 calories per 10 oz serving: 9 g protein, 1 g fat, 52 g carbohydrate; 52 mg sodium; 0 mg cholesterol.

Nutrition Highlights: Everyone knows oranges are rich sources of vitamin C. Many people don't realize that oranges are also a good source of calcium. But, you need to eat the whole food to get it. Most of the calcium is in the pulpy part of the fruit.
Nectar Note: Frozen bananas are a wonderful addition to smoothies. First, select bananas that are ripe but not over-ripe. Then peel them and store in a zip-lock bag in your freezer.

Pineapple Banana Orange Mango Smoothie

This creamy blend of three tropical fruits is hard to beat. And the fresh lemon juice really makes it.

1/3 cup orange frozen juice concentrate
1/4 cup Kern's® Apricot Mango Nectar
1 scoop (5 tablespoons) **Whole Nectar® Ultimate Soy**
    Protein Smoothie Mix
1/2 mango (peeled, pitted)
1/2 cup pineapple
1/2 banana
1 tablespoon fresh lemon juice
1-1/2 to 2 cups ice

Makes about 20 oz.

Place all ingredients in the Vita-Mix container in order listed. Secure the lid. Select Variable #1, turn to ON, and quickly increase speed to #10. Switch to HIGH. Run about 20 seconds until smooth. Use tamper, if necessary, to help circulate ingredients.

236 calories per 10 oz serving: 8 g protein, 1 g fat, 49 g carbohydrate; 43 mg sodium; 0 mg cholesterol.

Nutrition Highlights: Tropical fruits like pineapples and mangos are very nutritious and low calorie. Improved growing and shipping methods now make them much more available. If you know how to pick the best fruit you won't be disappointed. We have some tips in the back of the book that can help you.
Nectar Note: Kern's® products are available in most grocery stores.

Jamaican Mango Tangerine Smoothie

The distinctive flavor of tangerine adds extra zip to this orange. mango blend. Don't forget the nutmeg. Jamaicans wouldn't think of serving this without it.

1 cup Kern's® mango nectar
2 tablespoons Minute Maid® orange tangerine frozen
 juice concentrate
2 tablespoons Whole Nectar® Ultimate Soy
 Protein Smoothie Mix
1 sprinkle of nutmeg
1/2 mango (peeled, seed removed)
1-1/2 to 1-3/4 cups ice

Makes about 20 oz.

Place all ingredients in the Vita-Mix container in order listed. Secure the lid. Select Variable #1, turn to ON, and quickly increase speed to #10. Switch to HIGH. Run about 20 seconds until smooth. Use tamper, if necessary, to help circulate ingredients.

164 calories per 10 oz serving: 3 g protein, 0 g fat, 37 g carbohydrate; 35 mg sodium; 0 mg cholesterol.

Nutrition Highlights: A tangerine is actually a type of mandarin orange. Like all oranges, tangerines are rich in vitamin C.

Variations: If mangos aren't around, cantaloupe or peaches make a very good substitute.

Banana Julep Shake

You might fall in love, the way we have, with this delicious, creamy sweet banana shake with a hint of mint.

1 cup Whole Nectar® Vanilla Super Soymilk
   (see page 93 for recipe)
1/2 banana
6 fresh, small mint leaves
1/2 teaspoon fresh lime zest
1 to 1-1/4 cups ice

Makes about 16 oz.

Place all ingredients in the Vita-Mix container in order listed. Secure the lid. Select Variable #1, turn to ON, and quickly increase speed to #10. Switch to HIGH. Run about 20 seconds until smooth. Use tamper, if necessary, to help circulate ingredients.

101 calories per 8 oz serving: 7 g protein, 1 g fat, 17 g carbohydrate; 36 mg sodium; 0 mg cholesterol

Nutrition Highlights: Fresh herbs, like mint, are finally getting the health recognition they deserve. Research has shown that many herbs appear to have potent antioxidants that are quite active even in small amounts. With a Vita-Mix it's easy to blend up whole leaves without tedious pre-chopping. Many grocery stores have fresh mint. Or grow your own in a pot on a windowsill.

Passionate Cantaloupe Smoothie

Perfumy, rich passion fruit has an intense tropical flavor. Blended with orange, it's the perfect background for a mild, melon blend.

1/2 cup Minute Maid® orange passion frozen juice concentrate (partially thawed)
1/2 cup water
3 tablespoons Whole Nectar® Ultimate Soy Protein Smoothie Mix
1-1/2 cup frozen cantaloupe cubes

Makes about 16 oz.

Place all ingredients in the Vita-Mix container in order listed. Secure the lid. Select Variable #1, turn to ON, and quickly increase speed to #10. Switch to HIGH. Run about 20 seconds until smooth. Use tamper, if necessary, to help circulate ingredients.

188 calories per 8 oz serving: 6 g protein, 1 g fat, 41 g carbohydrate, 35 mg sodium; 0 mg cholesterol

Nectar Note: To partially thaw frozen juice concentrate, just scoop out the amount needed into a measuring cup and let it sit out for a few minutes until it's no longer totally frozen. Then you're ready to whirl. Or thaw out the whole frozen juice concentrate container in the refrigerator. Just use it up within a couple days.

Coco Guava Strawberry Shake

We think you'll enjoy this refreshing shake inspired by the popular Mexican *bebidas de coco y limon* (a tasty blend of coconut milk, fresh lime juice, fresh fruit and a little sweetening). If you use lite coconut milk, you'll dodge quite a few of the calories and still have a flavorful drink. We like the flavor and lower calorie of the Thai Kitchen® brand, but certainly you can use any kind that's available.

1/4 cup Thai Kitchen® lite coconut milk (unsweetened)
3/4 cup Kerns® Guava Nectar
1-1/2 teaspoons fresh lime juice
1-1/2 teaspoons Florida Crystals Natural Sugar
  (or other sugar)
1 tablespoon Whole Nectar® Ultimate Soy Protein Smoothie Mix
1/2 cup frozen strawberries (unsweetened)
1/2 to 3/4 cup ice

Makes about 16 oz

Place all ingredients in the Vita-Mix container in order listed. Secure the lid. Select Variable #1, turn to ON, and quickly increase speed to #10. Switch to HIGH. Run about 20 seconds until smooth. Use tamper, if necessary, to help circulate ingredients.

116 calories per 8 oz serving: 2 g protein, 2 g fat, 22 g carbohydrate; 28 mg sodium; 0 mg cholesterol

Nutrition Highlights: Guava fruit look like large, rumpled limes. But, don't be fooled by their rather curious outward appearance. Slice them open and you'll find a sweet smelling, pretty pink flesh rich in vitamin C and pectin, a type of fiber that appears to help lower blood cholesterol. **Nectar Note:** If you can't find lite coconut milk, just buy regular, use half the amount called for in the recipe and use water or nonfat milk to make up the other half.

Kiwi Pineapple Smoothie

Sometimes kiwi fruit can taste a little on the tart side. That makes them the perfect match for the sweetness of pineapple. Their combined flavors create a very refreshing lemon-lime!

1/3 cup pineapple frozen juice concentrate
1/3 cup water
1 scoop (5 tablespoons) **Whole Nectar® Ultimate Soy**
   Protein Smoothie Mix
2 kiwi fruit (peeled)
1-1/2 to 2 cups ice cubes

Makes about 20 oz.

Place all ingredients in the Vita-Mix container in order listed. Secure the lid. Select Variable #1, turn to ON, and quickly increase speed to #10. Switch to HIGH. Run about 20 seconds until smooth. Use tamper, if necessary, to help circulate ingredients.

192 calories per 10 oz serving: 9 g protein, 1 g fat, 38 g carbohydrate; 58 mg sodium; 0 mg cholesterol.

Nutrition Highlights: Ounce for ounce, kiwi fruit has more vitamin C than citrus fruit.

Orange Date Shake

Sweet dates are a delicious compliment for tangy orange juice in this energizing blend. Dates are a concentrated natural sugar so you don't need to use many. Next time you want to sweeten any of your blends, try dates instead of sugar or honey.

1-1/2 cups orange juice
3 pitted dates (or to taste)
1 scoop (5 tablespoons) **Whole Nectar® Ultimate Soy**
   Protein Smoothie Mix
1/2 - 1 cup ice

Makes about 20 oz.

Place all ingredients in the Vita-Mix container in order listed. Secure the lid. Select Variable #1, turn to ON, and quickly increase speed to #10. Switch to HIGH. Run about 30 seconds until smooth. Decrease speed to Variable #3 and run for about 20 seconds.

174 calories per 10 oz serving: 9 g protein, 1 g fat, 34 g carbohydrate; 42 mg sodium; 0 mg cholesterol

Nutrition Highlights: Dates and orange juice are both rich sources of potassium. There's strong evidence that a potassium rich diet helps prevent high blood pressure and reduces the risk of stroke and other cardiovascular diseases.
Variations: Instead of regular orange juice, try orange tangerine, orange passion or any other orange blend. Or add 1 small banana. Or add a sprinkle of nutmeg.

Grapefruit Strawberry Smoothie

If you're in the mood for a tangy pick-me-up, this smoothie might just do it. Red grapefruit juice is a zippy background for the sweetness of banana and strawberry.

1/3 cup red grapefruit frozen concentrate (thawed)
1/4 cup water
1 scoop (5 tablespoons) **Whole Nectar® Ultimate Soy Protein Smoothie Mix**
1/2 banana
3/4 cup frozen strawberries (unsweetened)
1 to 1-1/2 cups ice

Makes about 20 oz.

Place all ingredients in the Vita-Mix container in order listed. Secure the lid. Select Variable #1, turn to ON, and quickly increase speed to #10. Switch to HIGH. Run about 20 seconds until smooth. Use tamper, if necessary, to help circulate ingredients.

198 calories per 10 oz serving: 8 g protein, 1 g fat, 39 g carbohydrate; 73 mg sodium; 0 mg cholesterol.

Nutrition Highlights: Strawberries have more vitamin C than most berries and are one of the antioxidant champs.

Pineapple Coconut Smoothie

We consider any smoothie with a lot of pineapple to be like a mini-vacation! So, if you wish you were at the beach and just can't quite get there, close your eyes and sip this smoothie.

1/3 cup pineapple frozen juice concentrate
1/4 cup water
1 scoop (5 tablespoons) **Whole Nectar® Ultimate Soy Protein Smoothie Mix**
1 cup pineapple
1 tablespoon flaked coconut
1-1/4 to 1-3/4 cups ice

Makes about 20 oz.

Place all ingredients in the Vita-Mix container in order listed. Secure the lid. Select Variable #1, turn to ON, and quickly increase speed to #10. Switch to HIGH. Run about 20 seconds until smooth. Use tamper, if necessary, to help circulate ingredients.

201 calories per 10 oz serving: 8 g protein, 2 g fat, 37 g carbohydrate; 63 mg sodium; 0 mg cholesterol.

Nutrition Highlights: Pineapple contains an important digestive enzyme called bromelain. Much of it is in the core, so be sure to include that part of the fruit in your smoothie. The core is very fibrous but the Vita-Mix will smooth it right out.

Orange Strawberry Banana Smoothie

Definitely a classic, the orange, strawberry, banana smoothie is still a big favorite with many people. We've updated it from it's 70's roots, and brought it into the new nutrition millennium with the addition of healthy soy protein and whole foods.

1/3 cup orange frozen juice concentrate
1 teaspoon pure vanilla extract
1 scoop (5 tablespoons) **Whole Nectar® Ultimate Soy**
  Protein Smoothie Mix
1/4 cup Dannon® lowfat vanilla yogurt
1/2 banana
4 strawberries
1/2 orange (peeled)
1-1/2 to 2 cups ice

Makes about 24 oz.

Place all ingredients in the Vita-Mix container in order listed. Secure the lid. Select Variable #1, turn to ON, and quickly increase speed to #10. Switch to HIGH. Run about 20 seconds until smooth. Use tamper, if necessary, to help circulate ingredients.

234 calories per 12 oz serving: 10 g protein, 1 g fat, 45 g carbohydrate; 87 mg sodium; 2 mg cholesterol.

Nutrition Highlights: Lowfat and nonfat yogurt is a great addition to many smoothies. Make sure you get all the health benefits by selecting yogurt that contains active (live) yogurt cultures.

Banana Margarita Smoothie

Are your afternoon snack breaks getting pretty dull? Is everything too predictable? It doesn't have to be. Why not throw a Banana Margarita Smoothie party for you and the crew?

2 tablespoons Bacardi® margarita frozen concentrate
6 oz Yoplait® lemon yogurt
2 tablespoons Whole Nectar® Ultimate Soy
Protein Smoothie Mix
1 small banana
1 cup fresh pineapple
1-1/2 to 1-3/4 cups ice

Makes about 20 oz.

Place all ingredients in the Vita-Mix container in order listed. Secure the lid. Select Variable #1, turn to ON, and quickly increase speed to #10. Switch to HIGH. Run about 20 seconds until smooth. Use tamper, if necessary, to help circulate ingredients.

222 calories per 10 oz serving: 7 g protein, 2 g fat, 48 g carbohydrate; 58 mg sodium; 5 mg cholesterol.

Variations: Want more tang in your margarita? Add an additional teaspoon or two of margarita concentrate or fresh lime juice.

Blue Hawaiian Smoothie

We like to think of this smoothie as a fusion of different food cultures - tropical coconut meets mountain blueberry.

1 cup Thai Kitchen® lite, unsweetened coconut milk
(or other lite coconut milk)
2 tablespoons Whole Nectar® Ultimate Soy Protein Smoothie Mix
1 tablespoon Florida Crystals Natural Sugar
(or other sugar)
1 teaspoon fresh lime juice
1/2 cup frozen blueberries (unsweetened)
1/2 to 3/4 cup ice

Makes about 16 oz.

Place all ingredients in the Vita-Mix container in order listed. Secure the lid. Select Variable #1, turn to ON, and quickly increase speed to #10. Switch to HIGH. Run about 20 seconds until smooth. Use tamper, if necessary, to help circulate ingredients.

164 calories per 8 oz serving: 5 g protein, 8 g fat, 17 g carbohydrate; 47 mg sodium; 0 mg cholesterol

Nutrition Highlights: A coconut is a nut just like almonds and walnuts. Like almost all nuts, coconut meat is high in fat. But unlike most nuts, the fat in coconut is saturated. Research now indicates that the saturated fat in coconut doesn't do anything to blood cholesterol (that's a good thing) and that older studies linking coconut to health problems were flawed.

Date Oat Orange Smoothie

As a breakfast smoothie, this delicious combination is guaranteed to give you a running head-start on the day.

1/3 cup orange frozen juice concentrate
1/2 cup water
1 scoop (5 tablespoons) **Whole Nectar® Ultimate Soy Protein Smoothie Mix**
1/3 cup Dannon® lowfat vanilla yogurt
1/3 cup oatmeal (right out of box-no need to cook)
1/2 orange (peeled)
6 pitted dates
1-1/2 to 2 cups ice

Makes about 24 oz.

Place all ingredients in the Vita-Mix container in order listed. Secure the lid. Select Variable #1, turn to ON, and quickly increase speed to #10. Switch to HIGH. Run about 20 seconds until smooth. Use tamper, if necessary, to help circulate ingredients.

283 calories per 12 oz serving: 12 g protein, 2 g fat, 53 g carbohydrate; 77 mg sodium; 3 mg cholesterol.

Nutrition Highlights: Eat your oats! They're an excellent source of complex carbohydrates and have more protein than wheat and rice.

Peach Banana Grapefruit Smoothie

The tang of red grapefruit and the sweet of peach juice and banana combine in one of our favorite blends.

**1/3 cup Welch's® White Grape peach
    frozen juice concentrate**
1 scoop (5 tablespoons) **Whole Nectar® Ultimate Soy
    Protein Smoothie Mix**
1/2 small red grapefruit
1 small banana
1-1/2 to 2 cups ice

Makes about 20 oz.

Place all ingredients in the Vita-Mix container in order listed. Secure the lid. Select Variable #1, turn to ON, and quickly increase speed to #10. Switch to HIGH. Run about 20 seconds until smooth. Use tamper, if necessary, to help circulate ingredients.

261 calories per 10 oz serving: 9 g protein, 1 g fat, 57 g carbohydrate; 52 mg sodium; 0 mg cholesterol.

Nutrition Highlights: If you carefully segment your grapefruit and throw away the white pith, you're getting rid of one of the more potent cancer fighting phytochemicals around - limonoids. The white pith of all citrus fruit is rich in this substance.

Vanilla Orange Smoothie

To distinguish this smoothie from some of the other orange smoothies we make, we could refer to this one as the "Orange Julius® smoothie". There's a strong resemblance in flavor but no comparison in the nutrition.

1/2 cup orange frozen juice concentrate
1/3 cup water
2 teaspoons pure vanilla extract
1/2 tablespoon honey
1 scoop (5 tablespoons) **Whole Nectar® Ultimate Soy Protein Smoothie Mix**
1/4 cup Carnation® nonfat powdered milk
1/4 cup Dannon® lowfat vanilla yogurt
1/2 orange (peeled)
1-1/2 to 2 cups ice

Makes about 24 oz.

Place all ingredients in the Vita-Mix container in order listed. Secure the lid. Select Variable #1, turn to ON, and quickly increase speed to #10. Switch to HIGH. Run about 20 seconds until smooth. Use tamper, if necessary, to help circulate ingredients.

264 calories per 12 oz serving: 12 g protein, 1 g fat, 51 g carbohydrate; 108 mg sodium; 4 mg cholesterol.

Nutrition Highlights: Sorry Orange Julius®. The high protein smoothie mix, whole orange and yogurt make our smoothie about a zillion times more nutritious than yours.

Cantaloupe Peach Orange Smoothie

We wanted to call this smoothie Fuzzy Cantaloupe and then decided we'd better stick to the original name. But, whatever name you use, you'll discover there's nothing boring about this peach-melon blend.

**1/3 cup Bacardi® Real Fruit Fuzzy Navel
   frozen concentrate
1 scoop** (5 tablespoons) **Whole Nectar® Ultimate Soy
   Protein Smoothie Mix
1/2 cup cantaloupe** (optional-with some seeds)
1/2 orange (peeled)
1-1/4 to 1-3/4 cups ice

Makes about 20 oz.

Place all ingredients in the Vita-Mix container in order listed. Secure the lid. Select Variable #1, turn to ON, and quickly increase speed to #10. Switch to HIGH. Run about 20 seconds until smooth. Use tamper, if necessary, to help circulate ingredients.

169 calories per 10 oz serving: 8 g protein, 1 g fat, 33 g carbohydrate; 44 mg sodium; 0 mg cholesterol.

Nutrition Highlights: Many people eat pumpkin seeds, so it shouldn't seem odd to eat melon seeds, too. After all, melon and pumpkin are close relatives in the same botanical family. While very nutritious, go easy on them because seeds are high in fat just like nuts.
Nectar Note: Melon seeds have a mild flavor so you probably won't taste them and the Vita-Mix will thoroughly break them down and blend them into your smoothie.

Ruby Honeydew Shake

Red grapefruit juice is a colorful, sweet-tart background for one of our favorite breakfast shakes.

1 cup red grapefruit juice
1 tablespoon Whole Nectar® Ultimate Soy
  Protein Smoothie Mix
1 cup frozen honeydew melon cubes

Makes about 16 oz.

Place all ingredients in the Vita-Mix container in order listed. Secure the lid. Select Variable #1, turn to ON, and quickly increase speed to #10. Switch to HIGH. Run about 20 seconds until smooth. Use tamper, if necessary, to help circulate ingredients.

100 calories per 8 oz serving: 2 g protein, 0 g fat, 23 g carbohydrate; 48 mg sodium; 0 mg cholesterol

Nutrition Highlights: The redder the better when it comes to grapefruit. The red pulp means it's rich in lycopene, a carotenoid which may have many cancer fighting properties.

Banana Colada

No ordinary colada, our Banana Colada is powered by healthy soy protein and lite, unsweetened coconut milk.

1 cup Thai Kitchen® lite, unsweetened coconut milk
(or other lite coconut milk)
1 scoop (5 tablespoons) **Whole Nectar® Ultimate Soy Protein Smoothie Mix**
1 tablespoon Florida Crystals Natural Sugar
(or other sugar)
1/2 banana
1 cup fresh pineapple
1 to 1-1/4 cups ice

Makes about 20 oz.

Place all ingredients in the Vita-Mix container in order listed. Secure the lid. Select Variable #1, turn to ON, and quickly increase speed to #10. Switch to HIGH. Run about 20 seconds until smooth. Use tamper, if necessary, to help circulate ingredients.

244 calories per 10 oz serving:11 g protein, 9 g fat, 32 g carbohydrate; 71 mg sodium; 0 mg cholesterol

Nutrition Highlights: No valid study has ever linked coconut to any kind of health problem. That makes sense because many generations of polynesians lived long and healthy lives eating lots of it. It is high fat, though, so eat it in moderation and look for the lite, unsweetened coconut milks that are much lower in fat and calories.

Mango Papaya Yogurt Smoothie

Summer is usually the time you'll find fresh mango and papaya in abundance. Don't pass them up. Their delicious tropical flavors could make some of your favorite smoothies.

1/3 cup Dole® orange peach mango frozen juice concentrate
1 scoop (5 tablespoons) **Whole Nectar® Ultimate Soy Protein Smoothie Mix**
1/4 cup Yoplait® Tropical Peach Yogurt
(or any tropical fruit flavored yogurt)
1/2 cup mango
1/2 cup papaya
1-1/4 to 1-3/4 cups ice

Makes about 24 oz.

Place all ingredients in the Vita-Mix container in order listed. Secure the lid. Select Variable #1, turn to ON, and quickly increase speed to #10. Switch to HIGH. Run about 20 seconds until smooth. Use tamper, if necessary, to help circulate ingredients.

227 calories per 12 oz serving: 10 g protein, 1 g fat, 44 g carbohydrate; 83 mg sodium; 2 mg cholesterol.

Nutrition Highlights: Papaya is rich in cryptoxanthin, a key carotenoid, plus some vitamin C and folic acid. There are two varieties, the smaller, pear shaped Hawaiian and the larger Mexican. The Hawaiian is usually sweeter, but the Mexican variety is often cheaper. Picking a good papaya is an art. Check out our chart How To Pick The Best Fruit in the back of the book and find out how to be the expert.

Lemon Pineapple Smoothie

We discovered that lemon and pineapple were meant for each other. The lemon takes just a little of the sweetness edge off the pineapple creating one of our favorite blends. This smoothie even smells good!

1/2 cup pineapple juice
1 scoop (5 tablespoons) **Whole Nectar® Ultimate Soy Protein Smoothie Mix**
1/4 cup Yoplait® lemon yogurt
1 tablespoon fresh lemon juice
1 cup frozen pineapple chunks
3/4 to 1-1/4 cups ice

Makes about 20 oz.

Place all ingredients in the Vita-Mix container in order listed. Secure the lid. Select Variable #1, turn to ON, and quickly increase speed to #10. Switch to HIGH. Run about 20 seconds until smooth. Use tamper, if necessary, to help circulate ingredients.

197 calories per 10 oz serving: 10 g protein, 2 g fat, 35 g carbohydrate; 79 mg sodium; 5 mg cholesterol.

Nutrition Highlights: Adding yogurt to smoothies is a great way to give them a nutritional bump. Yogurt is a rich source of protein, calcium, riboflavin, phosphorous and B12. Make sure to buy yogurt labeled "active yogurt cultures". This friendly bacteria aids in digestion and helps maintain a healthy bacterial balance in the digestive tract.

Orange Pineapple Smoothie

Why start the day with plain, old orange juice when you can bump it up with pineapple and healthy soy protein.

1/3 cup orange frozen juice concentrate
1 scoop (5 tablespoons) **Whole Nectar® Ultimate Soy Protein Smoothie Mix**
1/2 orange (peeled)
3/4 cup pineapple
1-1/2 to 2 cups ice

Makes about 20 oz.

Place all ingredients in the Vita-Mix container in order listed. Secure the lid. Select Variable #1, turn to ON, and quickly increase speed to #10. Switch to HIGH. Run about 20 seconds until smooth. Use tamper, if necessary, to help circulate ingredients.

183 calories per 10 oz serving: 8 g protein, 1 g fat, 36 g carbohydrate; 41 mg sodium; 0 mg cholesterol.

Nutrition Highlights: Be sure to include the pineapple core in your smoothies. It's a rich source of bromelain, a digestive enzyme. You'll always pick the best pineapples if you follow our tips on the How To Pick The Best Fruit chart in the back of the book.

Cran-Tangerine Cantaloupe Smoothie

The tangy flavor of cranberry is a great background for cantaloupe. You can up the nutrition, and not affect the flavor of this smoothie, by using some of the cantaloupe seeds.

1/2 cup Ocean Spray® Cran-Tangerine liquid concentrate
1 scoop (5 tablespoons) **Whole Nectar® Ultimate Soy Protein Smoothie Mix**
3/4 cup cantaloupe
1-1/4 to 1-3/4 cups ice

Makes about 20 oz.

Place all ingredients in the Vita-Mix container in order listed. Secure the lid. Select Variable #1, turn to ON, and quickly increase speed to #10. Switch to HIGH. Run about 20 seconds until smooth. Use tamper, if necessary, to help circulate ingredients.

251 calories per 10 oz serving: 9 g protein, 1 g fat, 52 g carbohydrate; 52 mg sodium; 0 mg cholesterol.

Nutrition Highlights: The brilliant orange color of cantaloupe tells you it's a rich source of the phytochemical, beta-carotene. If you'd like to know a little more about phytochemicals, see our section Phyto Primer in the back of the book.

Orange Carrot Smoothie

Orange is a great flavor partner for carrot in this tasty smoothie that always reminds us of orange sherbet. Carrot is a "stealth" ingredient - you won't taste it, honest. Just use lots of ice. Any smoothie with carrot needs to be nice and cold.

1/3 cup orange frozen juice concentrate
1/2 cup water
1 teaspoon pure vanilla extract
1 tablespoon honey
1 scoop (5 tablespoons) **Whole Nectar® Ultimate Soy**
   Protein Smoothie Mix
1/4 cup Dannon® lowfat vanilla yogurt
1/2 cup baby carrots
1-1/4 to 1-3/4 cups ice

Makes about 20 oz.

Place all ingredients in the Vita-Mix container in order listed. Secure the lid. Select Variable #1, turn to ON, and quickly increase speed to #10. Switch to HIGH. Run about 20 seconds until smooth. Use tamper, if necessary, to help circulate ingredients.

214 calories per 10 oz serving: 10 g protein, 1 g fat, 41 g carbohydrate; 71 mg sodium; 2 mg cholesterol.

Nutrition Highlights: A recent study suggests that as little as 3.7 mg of beta-carotene per day (about 1/2 carrot) may reduce your risk of breast cancer by as much as 68% One 10 oz serving of this delicious smoothie will give you that beta-carotene insurance.
Nectar Note: If you've never used carrot in a smoothie before, start with very small amounts of baby carrots. When you discover you can't taste them, you'll have confidence in adding more.

Brazilian Shake

If you're a little bored with your morning orange juice, why not start the day the way many South Americans do. Brazilians, in particular, like to blend avocado with all kinds of fruit and vegetable juices. We've added soy protein and wheat germ to give this wonderful drink even more nutritional clout.

2 cups orange juice
1/2 small avocado (peeled & pitted)
4 dates (pitted)
2 tablespoons Whole Nectar® Ultimate Soy
   Protein Smoothie Mix
2 tablespoons toasted wheat germ
1 to 1-1/4 cups ice

Makes about 20 oz.

Place all ingredients in the Vita-Mix container in order listed. Secure the lid. Select Variable #1, turn to ON, and quickly increase speed to #10. Switch to HIGH. Run about 20 seconds until smooth. Use tamper, if necessary, to help circulate ingredients.

276 calories per 10 oz serving: 8 g protein, 8 g fat, 46 g carbohydrate; 23 mg sodium; 0 mg cholesterol.

Nutrition Highlights: Avocados are rich in healthy mono-unsaturated fat, potassium and folate.

Banana Pistachio Smoothie

Attention pistachio lovers! Whirl this! And if you go for the exotic, be sure to add the cardamom. If you're not familiar cardamom, there's just no way to describe it's unique sweetly, spicy flavor. You just have to try it. While we love the flavor of cardamom, we can also vouch for the fact that this smoothie is very good with or without it.

1 cup vanilla rice milk
1 scoop (5 tablespoons) **Whole Nectar® Ultimate Soy Protein Smoothie Mix**
1 small banana
1/2 cup roasted, shelled pistachios
1/2 teaspoon ground cardamom (optional)
1-1/4 to 1-1/2 cups ice

Makes about 20 oz.

Place all ingredients in the Vita-Mix container in order listed. Secure the lid. Select Variable #1, turn to ON, and quickly increase speed to #10. Switch to HIGH. Run about 20 seconds until smooth. Use tamper, if necessary, to help circulate ingredients.

349 calories per 10 oz serving: 16 g protein, 15 g fat, 39 g carbohydrate; 76 mg sodium; 0 mg cholesterol.

Nutrition Highlights: Pistachios are good sources of iron, thiamin and phosphorous.

Nectar Note: You can find ground cardamom in the spice aisle of almost any grocery store. If you try it and like the flavor, you might want to add a little to other smoothies with tropical fruit flavors like mango and papaya.

Fresh Lime & Pineapple Shake

Don't miss this energizing tropical shake with a hint of lime. Fresh lime juice enhances the flavor of pineapple and other tropical fruit. That's why, from Hawaii to Mexico to South America, you'll find this flavor combination in so many classic drinks.

3/4 cup Whole Nectar® Vanilla Super Soymilk
1/4 cup fresh lime juice
2 tablespoons Whole Nectar® Ultimate Soy
  Protein Smoothie Mix
1 banana
1/2 cup fresh pineapple
1 to 1-1/4 cups ice

Makes about 20 oz.

Place all ingredients in the Vita-Mix container in order listed. Secure the lid. Select Variable #1, turn to ON, and quickly increase speed to #10. Switch to HIGH. Run about 20 seconds until smooth. Use tamper, if necessary, to help circulate ingredients.

152 calories per 10 oz serving: 9 g protein, 1 g fat, 29 g carbohydrate; 44 mg sodium; 0 mg cholesterol

Nutrition Highlights: Fresh lime juice is a very rich source of vitamin C.
Nectar Note: Here's the easiest way to get the maximum amount of juice out of a lime: First, roll the lime back and forth on the counter, pressing hard with your palm. Then, slice the lime in half and use a citrus reaming tool to get all the juice. Room temperature limes will juice more easily than very cold ones.

Orange Almond Banana Smoothie

This energetically orange smoothie, with a burst of banana almond flavor, is a proud addition to our smoothie collection.

1/2 cup orange frozen juice concentrate
1/2 cup water
1 scoop (5 tablespoons) **Whole Nectar® Ultimate Soy Protein Smoothie Mix**
1 small banana
1 small orange (peeled & halved)
10 raw almonds
1/2 teaspoon almond extract
1-1/2 to 1-3/4 cups ice

Makes about 20 oz.

Place all ingredients in the Vita-Mix container in order listed. Secure the lid. Select Variable #1, turn to ON, and quickly increase speed to #10. Switch to HIGH. Run about 20 seconds until smooth. Use tamper, if necessary, to help circulate ingredients.

289 calories per 10 oz serving: 10 g protein, 4 g fat, 55 g carbohydrate; 41 mg sodium; 0 mg cholesterol

Nutrition Highlights: Don't sell orange juice concentrate short! It's just as nutritious as fresh juice. But as nutritious as orange juice is, it's no match for the nutrition in a whole orange. Besides vitamin C, oranges are a rich storehouse of a long list of health promoting substances. Many of these substances are found primarily in the white pith and fibrous part of the fruit. You don't get much of these nutrients if you just drink the juice.

Deluxe Orange Shake

Orange juice lovers will definitely want to try this very special orange treat, bursting with flavor and vitamin C. Use lowfat orange sherbet without partially hydrogenated oil as an ingredient.

1/2 cup orange juice
1 tablespoon Whole Nectar® Ultimate Soy
   Protein Smoothie Mix
1/2 orange (peeled)
1 cup lowfat orange sherbet

Makes about 12 oz.

Place all ingredients in the Vita-Mix container in order listed. Secure the lid. Select Variable #1, turn to ON, and quickly increase speed to #10. Switch to HIGH. Run about 20 seconds until smooth. Use tamper, if necessary, to help circulate ingredients.

166 calories per 6 oz serving: 3 g protein, 1 g fat, 37 g carbohydrate; 34 mg sodium; 0 mg cholesterol

Nutrition Highlights: Study after study has shown that people who eat the most vitamin C rich foods have less heart disease and cancer. But the operative word here is *food*. Taking vitamin C supplements doesn't seem to have the same effect. So, If you thought you were covered by taking supplements, you might want to reconsider. Vitamin C rich smoothies might just be some of your best health insurance.

Strawberry Daiquiri Smoothie

Smoothies don't always have to be sweet. Flavorful, stimulating and more tangy than sweet, the Strawberry Daiquiri Smoothie was created in the tradition of the classic Cuban drink (but without the rum, of course).

**1/3 cup Bacardi® Strawberry Daiquiri
   frozen concentrate**
3/4 cup water
2 tablespoons fresh lime juice
1 teaspoon fresh lime zest
1 scoop (5 tablespoons) **Whole Nectar® Ultimate Soy
   Protein Smoothie Mix**
1 cup frozen strawberries (unsweetened)
1 to 1-1/4 cups ice

Makes about 20 oz.

Place all ingredients in the Vita-Mix container in order listed. Secure the lid. Select Variable #1, turn to ON, and quickly increase speed to #10. Switch to HIGH. Run about 20 seconds until smooth. Use tamper, if necessary, to help circulate ingredients.

166 calories per 10 oz serving: 8 g protein, 1 g fat, 35 g carbohydrate; 53 mg sodium; 0 mg cholesterol

Nutrition Highlights: Even the tang is healthy! The substances in lime juice and zest that give them their tart flavor are also believed to be antioxidants with cancer fighting ability.

Orange Peach Mango Smoothie

When Dole® put the orange, peach, mango flavors together they were definitely on to something. Add the whole food nutrition of fresh mango and frozen peaches and you'll really be on to something, too.

**1/3 cup Dole® Orange Peach Mango
  frozen juice concentrate**
1/2 cup water
1 scoop (5 tablespoons) **Whole Nectar® Ultimate Soy
  Protein Smoothie Mix**
1/2 mango (about 1/2 cup)
1 cup frozen peach slices (unsweetened)
1 to 1-1/2 cups ice

Makes about 20 oz.

Place all ingredients in the Vita-Mix container in order listed. Secure the lid. Select Variable #1, turn to ON, and quickly increase speed to #10. Switch to HIGH. Run about 20 seconds until smooth. Use tamper, if necessary, to help circulate ingredients.

209 calories per 10 oz serving: 9 g protein, 1 g fat, 40 g carbohydrate; 65 mg sodium; 0 mg cholesterol.

Nutrition Highlights: Fresh mangos are plentiful and inexpensive during the spring and summer months. Try one. You could get hooked on their wonderful sweet taste and incredible nutrition. The 1/2 mango in this smoothie has an amazing 3894 IU of vitamin A !

Creamy Tropical Peach Yogurt Smoothie

Rich, sweet mangos are the world's most popular fruit and a perfect addition to a peach blend. The creamy consistency of this smoothie comes from blending frozen fruit, yogurt and not much ice.

6 oz. Yoplait® Tropical Peach Yogurt
2 tablespoons Bacardi® Fuzzy Navel
  frozen concentrate
2 tablespoons Whole Nectar® Ultimate Soy
  Protein Smoothie Mix
1/2 mango (peeled, seed removed)
1 cup frozen unsweetened peach slices
3/4 to 1 cup ice

Makes about 16 oz.

Place all ingredients in the Vita-Mix container in order listed. Secure the lid. Select Variable #1, turn to ON, and quickly increase speed to #10. Switch to HIGH. Run about 20 seconds until smooth. Use tamper, if necessary, to help circulate ingredients.

199 calories per 8 oz serving: 6 g protein, 1 g fat, 40 g carbohydrate; 57 mg sodium; 5 mg cholesterol.

Nutrition Highlights: Ounce for ounce, mangos have more beta carotene than cantaloupe, apricots or any other common fruit.

Nectar Note: Yoplait® Tropical Peach Yogurt is one of our favorites but any peach yogurt will make a very good smoothie.

Cherry Nectarine Smoothie

This rich tasting, sweet-tart blend of cherries and nectarines will fool you into thinking you're sipping some decadent dessert.

1/3 cup Welch's® Cherry Sensation
  liquid juice concentrate
1/4 cup water
1 scoop (5 tablespoons) **Whole Nectar® Ultimate Soy**
  Protein Smoothie Mix
1 nectarine (halved)
1 cup frozen cherries (Bing or other sweet variety)
1 to 1-1/2 cups ice

Makes about 24 oz.

Place all ingredients in the Vita-Mix container in order listed. Secure the lid. Select Variable #1, turn to ON, and quickly increase speed to #10. Switch to HIGH. Run about 20 seconds until smooth. Use tamper, if necessary, to help circulate ingredients.

231 calories per 12 oz serving: 9 g protein, 2 g fat, 50 g carbohydrate; 54 mg sodium; 0 mg cholesterol.

Nutrition Highlights: Fresh cherries are wonderful but the season is short. Frozen cherries are usually a more practical buy. Just be sure to buy a sweet variety like Bing or Lambert. Sour cherries (used in pies) actually have a little more vitamin C and beta-carotene than sweet, but are much too tart for smoothies.

Ginger Peach Cinnamon Smoothie

Fresh ginger is a wonderful addition to smoothies. If you have a Vita-Mix there's no tedious chopping or grating. Just peal the ginger and pop the whole piece in the Vita-Mix container. Fresh ginger pairs well with peaches, apples, pears and berries. Experiment with small amounts because a little goes a long way.

**1/3 cup Welch's® White Grape Peach
   frozen juice concentrate** (partially thawed)
1/2 cup water
**2 tablespoons Whole Nectar® Ultimate Soy
   Protein Smoothie Mix**
1 dime-sized piece fresh ginger (peeled)
   or 1/4 teaspoon ground ginger
1 sprinkle cinnamon
1 cup frozen peach slices (unsweetened)
1 to 1-1/4 cups ice

Makes about 16 oz.

Place all ingredients in the Vita-Mix container in order listed. Secure the lid. Select Variable #1, turn to ON, and quickly increase speed to #10. Switch to HIGH. Run about 20 seconds until smooth. Use tamper, if necessary, to help circulate ingredients.

154 calories per 8 oz serving: 4 g protein, 0 g fat, 33 g carbohydrate; 26 mg sodium; 0 mg cholesterol.

It's easy to keep fresh ginger on hand. Select fresh, firm ginger root. Dry well with a paper towel. Double wrap in aluminum foil (don't use plastic bag). Store in freezer. Slice off a small piece as needed, but don't thaw the rest of the root. Frozen ginger root will keep well for 6 to 9 months. *Or* store the root unwrapped (no bag or foil) on a rack in the refrigerator. Don't put it in a bin and don't pile items on top of it and it will keep well for as long as a month.

Apricot Strawberry Smoothie

Apricot and strawberry combine for a very refreshing, but not too sweet, smoothie. Since fresh apricots are often hard to find, we designed this smoothie to get it's apricot flavor from Kern's® apricot nectar and apricot flavored yogurt.

1/2 cup Kern's® apricot nectar
1 tablespoon honey
1 scoop (5 tablespoons) **Whole Nectar® Ultimate Soy Protein Smoothie Mix**
1/3 cup apricot lowfat yogurt
1 cup frozen strawberries (unsweetened)
3/4 to 1-1/4 cups ice

Makes about 20 oz.

Place all ingredients in the Vita-Mix container in order listed. Secure the lid. Select Variable #1, turn to ON, and quickly increase speed to #10. Switch to HIGH. Run about 20 seconds until smooth. Use tamper, if necessary, to help circulate ingredients.

184 calories per 10 oz serving: 9 g protein, 1 g fat, 35 g carbohydrate; 74 mg sodium; 1 mg cholesterol.

Nutrition Highlights: The color of apricots is a dead giveaway that they're another rich source of beta-carotene like carrots and cantaloupe.

Nectar Note: Kern's products can be found in most grocery stores.

Peach Oat Smoothie

This filling and tasty breakfast smoothie is genuinely a meal in a glass and one our favorites. We often add some rolled oats to a smoothie. They're a whole grain and ready to use right out of the box. Or use your leftover cooked cereal.

1/3 cup Welch's® White Grape Peach frozen juice concentrate
1/4 cup water
1 scoop (5 tablespoons) **Whole Nectar® Ultimate Soy Protein Smoothie Mix**
1/2 cup oatmeal (right out of box-no need to cook)
1 teaspoon flax seed
1 peach
1-1/2 to 2 cups ice

Makes about 20 oz.

Place all ingredients in the Vita-Mix container in order listed. Secure the lid. Select Variable #1, turn to ON, and quickly increase speed to #10. Switch to HIGH. Run about 20 seconds until smooth. Use tamper, if necessary, to help circulate ingredients.

297 calories per 10 oz serving: 12 g protein, 5 g fat, 51 g carbohydrate; 51 mg sodium; 0 mg cholesterol.

Nutrition Highlights: Flax seeds are a rich source of essential fatty acids and lignans (a phytochemical with a long list of healthful properties like lowering cholesterol and reducing menopausal symptoms). Flax seed oil does not contain lignans. The only way to get all the health benefits of these seeds is to grind them into flour or whip them up in the Vita-Mix like we do in this smoothie.

Orange Nectarine Mango Smoothie

If you're in the mood for a lightly tangy energy boost, try this smoothie. Nectarines are usually much more flavorful than peaches and make great smoothies. Nectarines and mangos are both inexpensive and widely available in the store during the summer months. Don't walk down the produce aisle without grabbing at least one of each.

1/3 cup orange frozen juice concentrate
1/4 cup water
1 scoop (5 tablespoons) **Whole Nectar® Ultimate Soy Protein Smoothie Mix**
1 nectarine (halved)
1/2 mango (peeled and pitted)
1-1/2 to 2 cups ice

Makes about 20 oz.

Place all ingredients in the Vita-Mix container in order listed. Secure the lid. Select Variable #1, turn to ON, and quickly increase speed to #10. Switch to HIGH. Run about 20 seconds until smooth. Use tamper, if necessary, to help circulate ingredients.

206 calories per 10 oz serving: 8 g protein, 1 g fat, 41 g carbohydrate; 42 mg sodium; 0 mg cholesterol.

Nutrition Highlights: Nectarines have more beta-carotene and vitamin A than peaches. Both orange juice and mango are rich in a carotenoid called zeaxanthin, a nutrient that's responsible for healthy eyes.

Peach Carrot Smoothie

Trust me on this. Peaches are the perfect cover for carrots. If you're not a big carrot lover, you can "sneak them in on yourself" in this smoothie.

**1/3 cup Welch's® White Grape Peach
  frozen juice concentrate**
1/2 cup water
1 tablespoon honey
1 scoop (5 tablespoons) **Whole Nectar® Ultimate Soy
  Protein Smoothie Mix**
6 baby carrots
3/4 cup frozen peach slices (unsweetened)
1 to 1-1/2 cups ice

Makes about 20 oz.

Place all ingredients in the Vita-Mix container in order listed.
Secure the lid. Select Variable #1, turn to ON, and quickly increase speed to #10. Switch to HIGH. Run about 20 seconds until smooth. Use tamper, if necessary, to help circulate ingredients.

235 calories per 10 oz serving: 8 g protein, 1 g fat, 48 g carbohydrate; 51 mg sodium; 0 mg cholesterol.

Nutrition Highlights: Carrots are one of the richest sources of the antioxidant beta-carotene and have loads of soluble fiber - two good reasons that carrot eaters tend to have far fewer heart attacks, strokes and cancer than carrot avoiders.

Peach Almond Spice Smoothie

This recipe is living proof that there's always a way to make a smoothie. Just keep a couple cans of fruit in the cupboard and you'll always be able to make something tasty and nutritious. Yes, canned is not quite as good for you as fresh (see below) but it's still nutritious. Besides, this smoothie tastes like peach pie. How can you turn that down?

1/3 cup Welch's® White Grape peach
frozen juice concentrate
1/8 teaspoon almond extract
1/2 teaspoon cinnamon
1 scoop (5 tablespoons) **Whole Nectar® Ultimate Soy**
Protein Smoothie Mix
1/2 can (15oz) **Del Monte® Harvest Spice**
sliced peaches with juice
1 to 1-1/2 cups ice

Makes about 20 oz.

Place all ingredients in the Vita-Mix container in order listed. Secure the lid. Select Variable #1, turn to ON, and quickly increase speed to #10. Switch to HIGH. Run about 20 seconds until smooth. Use tamper, if necessary, to help circulate ingredients.

225 calories per 10 oz serving: 8 g protein, 1 g fat, 47 g carbohydrate; 52 mg sodium; 0 mg cholesterol.

Nutrition Highlights: Canned fruit has less vitamin C and beta-carotene than fresh but it still nutritious. Just be sure to eat the juice with the fruit because a lot of the nutrients from the fruit dissolve into the liquid. Avoid the kind packed in heavy syrup.

Just Peach Smoothie

This is a basic, surefire, make-any-time smoothie. While fresh peaches are wonderful, frozen peach slices are very handy to have on hand.

1/3 cup Welch's® White Grape Peach frozen juice concentrate
1/2 cup water
1 scoop (5 tablespoons) **Whole Nectar® Ultimate Soy Protein Smoothie Mix**
1 cup frozen peach slices (unsweetened)
3/4 to 1-1/4 cups ice

Makes about 20 oz.

Place all ingredients in the Vita-Mix container in order listed. Secure the lid. Select Variable #1, turn to ON, and quickly increase speed to #10. Switch to HIGH. Run about 20 seconds until smooth. Use tamper, if necessary, to help circulate ingredients.

196 calories per 10 oz serving: 8 g protein, 1 g fat, 38 g carbohydrate; 51 mg sodium; 0 mg cholesterol.

Nutrition Highlights: Peaches are a good source of vitamin C and A.

Strawberry Peach Smoothie

Two favorite fruits blend into a wonderful high energy snack.

**1/3 cup Welch's® White Grape Peach
　　frozen juice concentrate**
1/2 cup water
1 tablespoon honey (optional)
1 scoop (5 tablespoons) **Whole Nectar® Ultimate Soy
　　Protein Smoothie Mix**
1/2 cup frozen strawberries (unsweetened)
1/2 cup frozen peaches (unsweetened)
3/4 to 1-1/4 cups ice

Makes about 20 oz.

Place all ingredients in the Vita-Mix container in order listed.
Secure the lid. Select Variable #1, turn to ON, and quickly increase
speed to #10. Switch to HIGH. Run about 20 seconds until smooth.
Use tamper, if necessary, to help circulate ingredients.

*226 calories per 10 oz serving: 8 g protein, 1 g fat, 47 g carbohydrate; 57
mg sodium; 0 mg cholesterol.*

Nutrition Highlights: Smoothies are a great way to make a dent in
those 5 to 9 servings of fruit and vegetables we should all eat every
day.

Banana Peach Nectarine Smoothie

This refreshing blend is guaranteed to give you a mid-morning boost.

**1/3 cup Welch's® White Grape Peach
   frozen juice concentrate**
1/4 cup water
1 scoop (5 tablespoons) **Whole Nectar® Ultimate Soy
   Protein Smoothie Mix**
1 peach (halved)
1 nectarine (halved)
1/2 banana
1-3/4 to 2-1/4 cups ice

Makes about 20 oz.

Place all ingredients in the Vita-Mix container in order listed.
Secure the lid. Select Variable #1, turn to ON, and quickly increase
speed to #10. Switch to HIGH. Run about 20 seconds until smooth.
Use tamper, if necessary, to help circulate ingredients.

*271 calories per 10 oz serving: 9 g protein, 1 g fat, 58 g carbohydrate; 52
mg sodium; 0 mg cholesterol.*

Nutrition Highlights: If you're in the habit of peeling everything,
stop and take a look at our To Peel Or Not To Peel section in the
back of the book. The peels of many fruits are very nutritious. The
peach and nectarine in this smoothie are examples of fruits that
don't need to be peeled.

Apricot Banana Oat Smoothie

Don't forget to keep some dried fruit on hand. Both dried apricots and peaches make knockout smoothies. This filling and delicious breakfast smoothie will definitely help you start the day in high gear.

3/4 cup Kern's® apricot nectar
1 scoop (5 tablespoons) **Whole Nectar® Ultimate Soy**
  Protein Smoothie Mix
1/3 cup oatmeal (right out of box-no need to cook)
1 small banana
6 halves dried apricot
1-1/2 to 2 cups ice

Makes about 20 oz.

Place all ingredients in the Vita-Mix container in order listed. Secure the lid. Select Variable #1, turn to ON, and quickly increase speed to #10. Switch to HIGH. Run about 20 seconds until smooth. Use tamper, if necessary, to help circulate ingredients.

253 calories per 10 oz serving: 10 g protein, 2 g fat, 49 g carbohydrate; 44 mg sodium; 0 mg cholesterol.

Nutrition Highlights: Dried apricots don't have near the vitamin C of fresh but are still good sources of beta-carotene, iron, niacin, potassium and fiber.

Nectar Note: If you're lucky enough to have fresh apricots, use 3 or 4 in this recipe instead of the dried.

Blueberry Orange Smoothie

We use blueberries in lots of different combinations but we still keep coming back to one of our favorite combinations - blueberry orange.

1/3 cup orange frozen juice concentrate
1/2 cup water
1 scoop (5 tablespoons) **Whole Nectar® Ultimate Soy Protein Smoothie Mix**
1 cup frozen blueberries (un sweetened)
3/4 to 1-1/4 cups ice

Makes about 20 oz.

Place all ingredients in the Vita-Mix container in order listed. Secure the lid. Select Variable #1, turn to ON, and quickly increase speed to #10. Switch to HIGH. Run about 20 seconds until smooth. Use tamper, if necessary, to help circulate ingredients.

178 calories per 10 oz serving: 8 g protein, 1 g fat, 34 g carbohydrate; 42 mg sodium; 0 mg cholesterol.

Nutrition Highlights: Oranges and blueberries are on every expert's top 10 antioxidant foods list. Don't let the scarcity of fresh blueberries stop you from making some really delicious and nutritious smoothies. Use frozen or canned.

Kiwi Strawberry Smoothie

The first time we sliced kiwi and strawberries together and topped them with yogurt, we knew we were in love. We discovered that the unique, sweet-tart flavor of kiwi matches perfectly with strawberry. And the flavors worked so well together, we knew it would make a great smoothie.

1/3 cup Bacardi® Real Fruit Strawberry Daiquiri frozen concentrate
1/2 cup water
1 scoop (5 tablespoons) **Whole Nectar® Ultimate Soy Protein Smoothie Mix**
1 kiwi fruit (peeled)
1 cup frozen strawberries (unsweetened)
1 to 1-1/2 cups ice

Makes about 20 oz.

Place all ingredients in the Vita-Mix container in order listed. Secure the lid. Select Variable #1, turn to ON, and quickly increase speed to #10. Switch to HIGH. Run about 20 seconds until smooth. Use tamper, if necessary, to help circulate ingredients.

194 calories per 10 oz serving: 8 g protein, 1 g fat, 41 g carbohydrate; 55 mg sodium; 0 mg cholesterol.

Nutrition Highlights: Kiwi has more vitamin C (by weight) than oranges. Now that they're grown extensively in California, they're inexpensive and widely available in supermarkets most of the year. They have an interesting tangy flavor that works well with berries and other fruits.

Guava Raspberry Smoothie

The flowery sweetness of guava is sometimes described as tasting like a combination of berries and melon. Lightly tart raspberries are the perfect partner for this sweet tropical fruit.

**1/3 cup Hawaii's Own® guava raspberry
    frozen concentrate
3/4 cup water
1 scoop** (5 tablespoons) **Whole Nectar® Ultimate Soy
    Protein Smoothie Mix
1 cup frozen raspberries** (unsweetened)
1 to 1-1/4 cups ice

Makes about 20 oz.

Place all ingredients in the Vita-Mix container in order listed. Secure the lid. Select Variable #1, turn to ON, and quickly increase speed to #10. Switch to HIGH. Run about 20 seconds until smooth. Use tamper, if necessary, to help circulate ingredients.

217 calories per 10 oz serving: 9 g protein, 1 g fat, 44 g carbohydrate; 40 mg sodium; 0 mg cholesterol

Nutrition Highlights: Low calorie, high fiber foods like raspberries, could be one your best friend if you're trying to maintain a healthy weight. High fiber foods make you feel full and break down slowly. This helps to keep your blood sugar and energy level on an even keel. You'll be more likely to pass up those high calorie, empty nutrition snacks.

Apple Berry Almond Smoothie

Apples and berries of any variety are a great flavor combination to mix and match. We particularly like to use sweet-tart Gala apples and blackberries.

1/3 cup apple frozen juice concentrate
1/2 cup vanilla almond milk
1 scoop (5 tablespoons) **Whole Nectar® Ultimate Soy Protein Smoothie Mix**
1/2 apple
1 cup frozen berries (unsweetened, any variety)
1 to 1-1/2 cups ice

Makes about 20 oz.

Place all ingredients in the Vita-Mix container in order listed. Secure the lid. Select Variable #1, turn to ON, and quickly increase speed to #10. Switch to HIGH. Run about 20 seconds until smooth. Use tamper, if necessary, to help circulate ingredients.

231 calories per 10 oz serving: 9 g protein, 2 g fat, 46 g carbohydrate; 70 mg sodium; 0 mg cholesterol.

Nutrition Highlights: You'll find almond milk in health food stores but why not make your own. See our recipe for Vanilla Almond Super Soymilk made with real almonds. It's easy to make if you have a Vita-Mix and very delicious.

Strawberry Banana Smoothie

This smoothie ought to be called the "potassium special" because both strawberries and bananas are loaded with this vital element.

1/3 cup apple frozen juice concentrate
1/2 cup water
1 scoop (5 tablespoons) **Whole Nectar® Ultimate Soy Protein Smoothie Mix**
1 banana
1 cup frozen strawberries (unsweetened)
1 to 1-1/2 cups ice

Makes about 20 oz.

Place all ingredients in the Vita-Mix container in order listed. Secure the lid. Select Variable #1, turn to ON, and quickly increase speed to #10. Switch to HIGH. Run about 20 seconds until smooth. Use tamper, if necessary, to help circulate ingredients.

249 calories per 10 oz serving: 8 g protein, 1 g fat, 54 g carbohydrate; 46 mg sodium; 0 mg cholesterol.

Nutrition Highlights: Potassium, a mineral that is lost during physical activity, is vital for controlling heartbeat, blood pressure and the body's fluid balance. A potassium rich diet has been proven to significantly reduce the risk of stroke.

Orange Blackberry Kiwi Smoothie

Think of this blend as more than a smoothie. You might want to call it your own private label, gourmet berry sorbet - thick and creamy, brilliant violet color and great taste. We're not food "scientists", but we think there's something in ligh y tangy kiwi fruit that actually enhances the flavor of blackberries.

1 cup vanilla rice milk
2 tablespoons orange frozen juice concentrate
2 tablespoons Whole Nectar® Ultimate Soy
   Protein Smoothie Mix
1 kiwi (peeled)
1 cup frozen blackberries (unsweetened)

Makes about 16 oz.

Place all ingredients in the Vita-Mix container in order listed. Secure the lid. Select Variable #1, turn to ON, and quickly increase speed to #10. Switch to HIGH. Run about 20 seconds until smooth. Use tamper, if necessary, to help circulate ingredients.

183 calories per 8 oz serving: 5 g protein, 1 g fat, 39 g carbohydrate; 63 mg sodium; 0 mg cholesterol

Variations: Instead of rice milk try using vanilla soymilk or oat milk. Orange tangerine frozen juice concentrate is very good instead of regular orange juice concentrate.

Nectar Note: Very fresh blackberries are extremely delicious but are also very fragile and perishable. Use fresh when you can, but frozen are just as nutritious and much more practical.

Vanilla Blueberry Banana Smoothie

We never tire of this simple but very tasty blend. No ice is necessary in this recipe. The frozen blueberries do all the chilling.

1 cup vanilla rice milk
2 tablespoons Whole Nectar® Ultimate Soy
  Protein Smoothie Mix
1/2 banana
3/4 cup frozen blueberries (unsweetened)

Makes about 16 oz.

Place all ingredients in the Vita-Mix container in order listed. Secure the lid. Select Variable #1, turn to ON, and quickly increase speed to #10. Switch to HIGH. Run about 20 seconds until smooth. Use tamper, if necessary, to help circulate ingredients.

135 calories per 8 oz serving: 5 g protein, 1 g fat, 28 g carbohydrate; 52 mg sodium; 0 mg cholesterol.

Variations: Instead of rice milk try using vanilla soymilk, oat milk or almond milk.

Cranberry Strawberry Smoothie

This smoothie is an example of what we call a "two berry" - put any two berries together and you're bound to create a really good smoothie. Cranberry and strawberry are just one of many delicious combinations.

1/3 cup cranberry juice frozen concentrate (thawed)
1/4 cup water
1 scoop (5 tablespoons) **Whole Nectar® Ultimate Soy Protein Smoothie Mix**
1 cup frozen strawberries (unsweetened)
3/4 to to 1-1/2 cups ice

Makes about 20 oz.

Place all ingredients in the Vita-Mix container in order listed. Secure the lid. Select Variable #1, turn to ON, and quickly increase speed to #10. Switch to HIGH. Run about 20 seconds until smooth. Use tamper, if necessary, to help circulate ingredients.

185 calories per 10 oz serving: 8 g protein, 1 g fat, 37 g carbohydrate; 53 mg sodium; 0 mg cholesterol.

Nutrition Highlights: Strawberries are nutrition dense packages that have more vitamin C ounce for ounce than oranges and grapefruit. They also contain a substance called ellagic acid which may help to prevent certain cancers.

Apple Melon Smoothie

This smoothie is a delicious way to use your favorite melons. We like to use cantaloupe and orange honeydew in this one.

1/3 cup apple frozen juice concentrate
1 tablespoon honey
1 scoop (5 tablespoons) **Whole Nectar® Ultimate Soy Protein Smoothie Mix**
2 cups melon (any kind or combination)
  with seeds for added nutrition
1-3/4 to 2-1/4 cups ice

Makes about 20 oz.

Place all ingredients in the Vita-Mix container in order listed. Secure the lid. Select Variable #1, turn to ON, and quickly increase speed to #10. Switch to HIGH. Run about 20 seconds until smooth. Use tamper, if necessary, to help circulate ingredients.

227 calories per 10 oz serving: 9 g protein, 1 g fat, 47 g carbohydrate; 58 mg sodium; 0 mg cholesterol.

Nutrition Highlights: Melons are a good source of potassium and vitamin C. The orange fleshed ones like cantaloupe have impressive amounts of beta-carotene. Use some of the seeds in your smoothies. They're very nutritious. The Vita-Mix will smooth them out and you won't taste them.

Strawberry Guava Mango Smoothie

Frozen strawberries are a staple item in our freezer. They mix and match with almost any frozen juice concentrate you have on hand to make wonderful, nutritious smoothies at the drop of a hat. In this case, the strawberries blended in a tropical fruit background, are a great pairing. Have fun creating your own custom combinations.

1/3 cup Chiquita® Pine-Guava-Mango frozen juice concentrate
1/2 cup water
1 scoop (5 tablespoons) **Whole Nectar® Ultimate Soy Protein Smoothie Mix**
1 cup frozen strawberries (unsweetened)
3/4 to 1-1/4 cups ice

Makes about 20 oz.

Place all ingredients in the Vita-Mix container in order listed. Secure the lid. Select Variable #1, turn to ON, and quickly increase speed to #10. Switch to HIGH. Run about 20 seconds until smooth. Use tamper, if necessary, to help circulate ingredients.

172 calories per 10 oz serving: 9 g protein, 1 g fat, 34 g carbohydrate; 67 mg sodium; 0 mg cholesterol.

Nutrition Highlights: Studies show that frozen fruit is usually just as or more nutritious than supermarket fresh fruit. The reason: fruit that's harvested for freezing is picked at the height of ripeness and flash frozen right from the field. Fresh fruit, on the other hand, is often picked green, and then subjected to storage and travel before it gets to you.

Mountain Blueberry Smoothie

What do bears and the scientists at Tufts University Research Center on Aging have in common? Both groups can't stay away from the blueberries now that they know about the power of their antioxidant, anti-aging properties.

**1/3 cup Welch's® White Grape Raspberry
    frozen juice concentrate**
1/2 cup water
1 tablespoon honey (optional)
1 scoop (5 tablespoons) **Whole Nectar® Ultimate Soy
    Protein Smoothie Mix**
1 cup frozen blueberries (unsweetened)
3/4 to 1-1/4 cups ice

Makes about 20 oz.

Place all ingredients in the Vita-Mix container in order listed. Secure the lid. Select Variable #1, turn to ON, and quickly increase speed to #10. Switch to HIGH. Run about 20 seconds until smooth. Use tamper, if necessary, to help circulate ingredients.

237 calories per 10 oz serving: 8 g protein, 1 g fat, 49 g carbohydrate; 52 mg sodium; 0 mg cholesterol.

Nutrition Highlights: Blueberries have more antioxidant punch than any other common fruit or vegetable.

Razzleberry Pie Smoothie

Our inspiration for this smoothie came from the Marie Callendar's® pie of the same name. We think Marie would be pleased with the smoothie inspired by her flavorful pie.

1 cup apple juice
2 tablespoons Whole Nectar® Ultimate Soy
  Protein Smoothie Mix
1/2 tart apple (like Granny Smith)
1/4 cup frozen raspberries (unsweetened)
1/2 cup frozen blackberries (unsweetened)
1 to 1-1/4 cups ice

Makes about 20 oz.
raspberry newtons (for optional "crust")

Place all ingredients, *except newtons*, in the Vita-Mix container in order listed. Secure the lid. Select Variable #1, turn to ON, and quickly increase speed to #10. Switch to HIGH. Run about 20 seconds until smooth. Use tamper, if necessary, to help circulate ingredients. *To make optional "crust":* Make smoothie thick so that you can eat it with a spoon. Pour smoothie into glass. Crumble newtons on top to make "crust".

158 calories per 10 oz serving: 6 g protein, 1 g fat, 33 g carbohydrate; 25 mg sodium; 0 mg cholesterol (without newtons)

Nutrition Highlights: Fiber rich foods, like berries and apples, are also low calorie, low fat and nutrient dense. It's all part of a healthy package deal you get with high fiber foods. You don't need to be an expert on all the fine points of nutrition to eat healthfully. Just eat a wide variety of high fiber, whole foods and the fine points will take care of themselves.

Strawberry Cranberry Raspberry Smoothie

Revive yourself with this colorful sweet-tart smoothie. It'll perk you up just looking at it!

1/3 cup cranberry frozen juice concentrate
1/4 cup water
1 scoop (5 tablespoons) **Whole Nectar® Ultimate Soy Protein Smoothie Mix**
1/2 cup strawberry lowfat yogurt
1 cup frozen raspberries (unsweetened)
3/4 to 1-1/4 cups ice

Makes about 20 oz.

Place all ingredients in the Vita-Mix container in order listed. Secure the lid. Select Variable #1, turn to ON, and quickly increase speed to #10. Switch to HIGH. Run about 20 seconds until smooth. Use tamper, if necessary, to help circulate ingredients.

281 calories per 10 oz serving: 11 g protein, 1 g fat, 55 g carbohydrate; 78 mg sodium; 4 mg cholesterol.

Nutrition Highlights: Unfortunately, fresh raspberries are both expensive and very perishable. Buying them frozen is the ideal way to keep this delicious and nutritious berry on hand. All the berries in this smoothie are rich sources of the cancer fighting substance ellagic acid.

Apple Granola Smoothie

Apples and granola make a very tasty and comforting breakfast smoothie. And, not only can you sip it, you can also pour it over granola in a bowl and eat it with a spoon!

1/3 cup apple juice concentrate
1/3 cup water
1 teaspoon pure vanilla extract
1 scoop (5 tablespoons) **Whole Nectar® Ultimate Soy Protein Smoothie Mix**
1 teaspoon cinnamon
1/3 cup lowfat granola
1 apple (halved)
1-1/2 to 2 cups ice

Makes about 20 oz.

Place all ingredients in the Vita-Mix container in order listed. Secure the lid. Select Variable #1, turn to ON, and quickly increase speed to #10. Switch to HIGH. Run about 20 seconds until smooth. Use tamper, if necessary, to help circulate ingredients.

320 calories per 10 oz serving: 10 g protein, 2 g fat, 68 g carbohydrate; 49 mg sodium; 0 mg cholesterol.

Nutrition Highlights: While more flamboyant foods grab the health press, the apple continues to be a steady source of fiber, potassium, boron and other nutrients. But, only if you eat the whole food. Much of the nutrition is in the peel and the fibrous part of the fruit.

Stealth Nut Smoothie

The Vita-Mix machine can make a very stealthy smoothie! Under the cover of a very tasty, fruity, orange-blueberry flavored blend, look at all the other nutritious foods we were able to sneak in undetected. The power of the machine thoroughly breaks down and blends every element - even small seeds like flax.

1/3 cup orange frozen juice concentrate
1/2 cup water
2 tablespoons Whole Nectar® Ultimate Soy
   Protein Smoothie Mix
1/2 teaspoon *each* **flax seed and toasted wheat germ**
1 teaspoon sunflowers seeds
1 tablespoon raw almonds
1/4 orange, 1/4 apple, 1/4 banana (small)
1/2 medium carrot, 1 medium lettuce leaf
3 frozen strawberries, 1/2 cup frozen blueberries
1/2 to 3/4 cup ice
Makes about 20 oz.

Place all ingredients in the Vita-Mix container in order listed. Secure the lid. Select Variable #1, turn to ON, and quickly increase speed to #10. Switch to HIGH. Run about 20 seconds until smooth. Use tamper, if necessary, to help circulate ingredients.

199 calories per 10 oz serving: 6 g protein, 4 g fat, 36 g carbohydrate; 17 mg sodium; 0 mg cholesterol

Nectar Note: Be creative. Make your own custom Stealth Nut Smoothie. The secret is to use small amounts of foods and carefully test each addition before adding more items. And to be a true Stealth Nut Smoothie it has to be tasty.

Deep Purple Smoothie

If you're a kid or would just like to feel like one, this smoothie is for you. It's just grapes - simple, straightforward and really delicious.

1/3 cup grape frozen juice concentrate
1/4 cup water
1 scoop (5 tablespoons) **Whole Nectar® Ultimate Soy Protein Smoothie Mix**
1 cup seedless grapes (preferably red)
1-1/4 to 1-3/4 cups ice

Makes about 20 oz.

Place all ingredients in the Vita-Mix container in order listed. Secure the lid. Select Variable #1, turn to ON, and quickly increase speed to #10. Switch to HIGH. Run about 20 seconds until smooth. Use tamper, if necessary, to help circulate ingredients.

181 calories per 10 oz serving: 8 g protein, 1 g fat, 36 g carbohydrate; 45 mg sodium; 0 mg cholesterol.

Nutrition Highlights: Grape skins are a rich source of resveratrol, a natural fungicide that slows the build up of LDL (bad) cholesterol. In addition, in a recent study of cancer prevention compounds in hundreds of plants, resveratrol came up the big winner.

Apple Banana Yogurt Smoothie

This mellow smoothie isn't flashy, but it's simple taste may be just the healthy refreshment you're looking for.

1/3 cup apple frozen juice concentrate
1/4 cup water
1 scoop (5 tablespoons) **Whole Nectar® Ultimate Soy Protein Smoothie Mix**
1/4 cup lowfat banana yogurt
1/2 apple
1 small frozen banana
1 to 1-1/2 cups ice

Makes about 20 oz.

Place all ingredients in the Vita-Mix container in order listed. Secure the lid. Select Variable #1, turn to ON, and quickly increase speed to #10. Switch to HIGH. Run about 20 seconds until smooth. Use tamper, if necessary, to help circulate ingredients.

239 calories per 10 oz serving: 9 g protein, 1 g fat, 48 g carbohydrate; 65 mg sodium; 2 mg cholesterol.

Nutrition Highlights: Apples are high in pectin, a soluble fiber known to lower cholesterol.

Nectar Note: If you find yourself with an abundance of bananas, why not freeze some for smoothies. Before they get too ripe, peel them and freeze in a quality storage bag.

Pear Apple Smoothie

It's too bad the fresh pear season is so short. They make a great smoothie. We especially like the combination of a sweet ripe pear and a tart apple like Granny Smith.

**1/3 cup Welch's® White Grape Pear
    frozen juice concentrate**
1 tablespoon apple frozen juice concentrate
1/4 cup water
1 scoop (5 tablespoons) **Whole Nectar® Ultimate Soy
    Protein Smoothie Mix**
1 pear (halved)
1/2 apple
1-1/4 to 1-3/4 cups ice

Makes about 20 oz.

Place all ingredients in the Vita-Mix container in order listed. Secure the lid. Select Variable #1, turn to ON, and quickly increase speed to #10. Switch to HIGH. Run about 20 seconds until smooth. Use tamper, if necessary, to help circulate ingredients.

250 calories per 10 oz serving: 8 g protein, 1 g fat, 53 g carbohydrate; 52 mg sodium; 0 mg cholesterol.

Nutrition Highlights: The pear, like it's botanical cousin the apple, is a good source of vitamin C and fiber. But only if you eat the whole food. Most of the vitamin C in a pear is in the skin.

Cranberry Orange Smoothie

Don't wait for Thanksgiving to whip up this refreshing smoothie. When fresh cranberries are available in the fall, buy a couple bags and throw them in your freezer so you're ready to make this smoothie anytime.

1/2 cup cranberry frozen juice concentrate
2 tablespoons orange juice concentrate
1 scoop (5 tablespoons) **Whole Nectar® Ultimate Soy Protein Smoothie Mix**
1 orange (halved)
1/4 cup whole berry cranberry sauce
    (or 1/2 cup frozen cranberries & honey to taste)
1-1/4 to 1-3/4 cups ice

Makes about 20 oz.

Place all ingredients in the Vita-Mix container in order listed. Secure the lid. Select Variable #1, turn to ON, and quickly increase speed to #10. Switch to HIGH. Run about 20 seconds until smooth. Use tamper, if necessary, to help circulate ingredients.

279 calories per 10 oz serving: 8 g protein, 1 g fat, 60 g carbohydrate; 67 mg sodium; 0 mg cholesterol.

Nutrition Highlights: Cranberries, like raspberries, strawberries, and grapes, contain ellagic acid, a substance that blocks the body's production of enzymes that cancer cells need to grow. Ellagic acid doesn't break down during cooking so cranberry sauce is a source as well as fresh cranberries.

Peach Raspberry Smoothie

Frozen peaches, like frozen strawberries, should be a staple item in your freezer. That way, a nutritious smoothie treat or mini-meal is only a quick whirl away.

1/3 cup Welch's® White Grape Raspberry
frozen juice concentrate
1/2 cup water
1 tablespoon honey (optional)
1 scoop (5 tablespoons) **Whole Nectar® Ultimate Soy**
Protein Smoothie Mix
1 cup frozen sliced peaches (unsweetened)
3/4 to 1-1/4 cups ice

Makes about 20 oz.

Place all ingredients in the Vita-Mix container in order listed. Secure the lid. Select Variable #1, turn to ON, and quickly increase speed to #10. Switch to HIGH. Run about 20 seconds until smooth. Use tamper, if necessary, to help circulate ingredients.

228 calories per 10 oz serving: 8 g protein, 1 g fat, 45 g carbohydrate; 51 mg sodium; 0 mg cholesterol.

Nutrition Highlights: Peaches are very low calorie and a good source of vitamin C and A.

Grape Berry Smoothie

Two fruits that deserve to be called nutritional super foods, combine for super taste. With grape as a background, any berry is good but blueberries are our favorite.

1/3 cup grape frozen juice concentrate
1/4 cup water
1 scoop (5 tablespoons) **Whole Nectar® Ultimate Soy Protein Smoothie Mix**
1 cup frozen, unsweetened berries
(any kind or combination)
3/4 to 1-1/4 cups ice

Makes about 20 oz.

Place all ingredients in the Vita-Mix container in order listed. Secure the lid. Select Variable #1, turn to ON, and quickly increase speed to #10. Switch to HIGH. Run about 20 seconds until smooth. Use tamper, if necessary, to help circulate ingredients.

200 calories per 10 oz serving: 9 g protein, 1 g fat, 40 g carbohydrate; 45 mg sodium; 0 mg cholesterol.

Nutrition Highlights: Both berries and grapes are loaded with ellagic acid, a natural substance that appears to have significant anti-cancer properties.

Fruit Salad Smoothie

The fruit salad smoothie is an artful combination of whatever you have around. Certainly, there are endless combinations and this is just one of them. There are two keys to making a good fruit salad: don't get too carried away with the variety of fruit and use small amounts of each ingredient.

1/3 cup orange juice
2 tablespoons Welch's® Cherry Sensation
   frozen juice concentrate
2 tablespoons pineapple juice
1 scoop (5 tablespoons) **Whole Nectar® Ultimate Soy**
   Protein Smoothie Mix
1 strawberry
1 slice each of apple, orange, nectarine
1 small piece of banana
1-1/2 to 2 cups ice

Makes about 24 oz.

Place all ingredients in the Vita-Mix container in order listed. Secure the lid. Select Variable #1, turn to ON, and quickly increase speed to #10. Switch to HIGH. Run about 20 seconds until smooth. Use tamper, if necessary, to help circulate ingredients.

174 calories per 12 oz serving: 9 g protein, 1 g fat, 34 g carbohydrate; 53 mg sodium; 0 mg cholesterol.

Nutrition Highlights: Eating a variety of whole foods is vital to your health and a varied diet starts at the supermarket. Buy small amounts of a wide variety of produce and vary your selections from week to week.

Cherry Grape Smoothie

This smoothie tastes as good as it sounds and then some. Our P.E.P.O.E. (Picky Eater Panel Of Experts) smoothie focus group named it as one of their favorites.

1/4 cup Welch's® Juicemakers grape liquid juice concentrate
1/4 cup Welch's® Cherry Sensation liquid juice concentrate
1 scoop (5 tablespoons) **Whole Nectar® Ultimate Soy Protein Smoothie Mix**
1/2 cup sweet cherries (Bing, Lambert)
1/2 cup red seedless grapes
1-1/4 to 1-3/4 cups ice

Makes about 20 oz.

Place all ingredients in the Vita-Mix container in order listed. Secure the lid. Select Variable #1, turn to ON, and quickly increase speed to #10. Switch to HIGH. Run about 20 seconds until smooth. Use tamper, if necessary, to help circulate ingredients.

252 calories per 10 oz serving: 8 g protein, 1 g fat, 54 g carbohydrate; 61 mg sodium; 0 mg cholesterol.

Nutrition Highlights: Grapes are nutrient dense and antioxidant rich. They contain a variety of compounds that do everything from preventing damage to cells, retarding tumor growth and benefiting blood cholesterol. Many of the healthy properties in grapes are in the skin so be sure to eat the whole food.

Blackberry Banana Smoothie

The depth of peach orange flavor in Bacardi® Fuzzy Navel frozen concentrate makes it a wonderful base for smoothies. In this smoothie it's a tasty peach background for rich blackberries.

1/3 cup Bacardi® Fuzzy Navel frozen concentrate
3/4 cup water
1 scoop (5 tablespoons) **Whole Nectar® Ultimate Soy**
   Protein Smoothie Mix
1 banana
1/2 cup frozen blackberries (unsweetened)
1-1/2 to 1-3/4 cups ice

Makes about 20 oz.

Place all ingredients in the Vita-Mix container in order listed. Secure the lid. Select Variable #1, turn to ON, and quickly increase speed to #10. Switch to HIGH. Run about 20 seconds until smooth. Use tamper, if necessary, to help circulate ingredients.

210 calories per 10 oz serving: 9 g protein, 1 g fat, 45 g carbohydrate; 41 mg sodium; 0 mg cholesterol

Nutrition Highlights: The dark violet color of blackberries comes from the phytochemical anthocyanidin in the fruit. Anthocyanidin is a potent antioxidant that may protect against heart disease. In addition, blackberries are rich in soluble fiber which helps to regulate cholesterol and the body's use of sugars.

Blueberry Yogurt Spice Smoothie

In a recent study, blueberries were impressive in their ability to reverse memory loss in old rats. We make a lot of blueberry smoothies and are hoping that what worked for the rats will work for us! This smoothie is hard to beat, especially if you like blueberry pie or blueberry pancakes.

3/4 cup nonfat milk
2 teaspoons maple syrup
1/2 teaspoon cinnamon
1 scoop (5 tablespoons) **Whole Nectar® Ultimate Soy**
   Protein Smoothie Mix
1/4 cup lowfat blueberry yogurt
3/4 cup frozen blueberries (unsweetened)
1 to 1-1/2 cups ice

Makes about 20 oz.

Place all ingredients in the Vita-Mix container in order listed. Secure the lid. Select Variable #1, turn to ON, and quickly increase speed to #10. Switch to HIGH. Run about 20 seconds until smooth. Use tamper, if necessary, to help circulate ingredients.

173 calories per 10 oz serving: 12 g protein, 1 g fat, 28 g carbohydrate; 109 mg sodium; 3 mg cholesterol.

Nutrition Highlights: The deep blue color in blueberries comes from anthocyanin, a powerful antioxidant.

Soymilk . . . .
Two reasons why you should make your own with Whole Nectar Ultimate Soy Protein Smoothie Mix.

More Protein

We call it super soymilk because it has *more than twice the protein* of it's nearest competitor.

See for yourself:

Silk® Soymilk (8 oz.)   6 g protein
Whole Nectar Super Soymilk (8 oz.) 14 g protein

In addition, our super soymilk has more than twice the calcium and less fat than the commercial brands.

Custom Blending

Are you buying Silk®, Westsoy® or any of the other popular brands of soymilk? They're good, but they have to be a "one taste fits all" product to be on the shelf in a store. With Whole Nectar Ultimate Soy Smoothie Mix, it's quick and easy to make the soymilk you want when you want it. Your custom blend will have the sweetening and other flavors to your own personal taste. Make as little or as much as you want and store in the refrigerator for up to 5 days.

And Whole Nectar super soymilk is creamy and delicious. So, what more could you want? Why not whirl some up today.

What is soymilk anyway?

Because the word "milk" is in the name, some people try soymilk for the first time and are surprised when it doesn't taste like cow's milk. But, think about it, a cow and a soybean are pretty different. So it makes sense that the milk they produce wouldn't have much in common. Just so you know what to expect, soymilk is best described as having a sweet, mildly nutty flavor.

In addition, while cow's milk and soymilk are both very nutritious, their profiles are quite different - one product being of animal origin and the other from a plant.

If you'd like to try some milk without the moo, may we recommend our Whole Nectar Vanilla Super Soymilk? We're very proud of our product because milking a bean is much harder than milking a cow.

**More About
Super Soymilk . . .**
Like all soymilk, Whole Nectar Super Soymilk needs to be shaken well before serving and should be served very cold. It's tasty all by itself or it can be an important ingredient in all kinds of shakes and smoothies.

In addition, you can cook with it and it makes great hot drinks.

Soymilk is light, refreshing and very tasty.
With a frosty cold bottle of Whole Nectar Super
Soymilk in your refrigerator, you always
have an energizing snack ready-to-go.

Vanilla Super Soymilk

Whirl this and you'll have delicious soymilk with more than twice the protein of the popular commercial brands. Just blend it up, chill, and like all soymilk, shake well before serving. Pour yourself a glass anytime or use it as the base for energizing shakes and smoothies. With Vanilla Super Soymilk on hand, you can jumpstart your morning with a *Mexican Coffee Shake* or take a break with a *Banana Julep.*

2 cups water
2 teaspoons pure vanilla extract
2 tablespoons Florida Crystals Natural Sugar
(or other sugar)
2/3 cup (2 scoops) **Whole Nectar® Ultimate Soy Protein Smoothie Mix**

Makes 18 oz.

Place all ingredients in the Vita-Mix container in order listed. Secure the lid. Select Variable #1, turn to ON, and quickly increase speed to #10. Run about 20 seconds until smooth. Decrease speed back down to Variable #3 and run about 10 seconds. Turn to OFF. Refrigerate and serve well-chilled. Shake well before serving.

149 calories per 8 oz serving: 14 g protein, 1 g fat, 21 g carbohydrate; 71 mg sodium; 0 mg cholesterol.

Nectar Note: Make your own custom blend of Super Soymilk by adjusting the vanilla and the sweetening up or down to suit your own tastes. We like the taste of the Florida Crystals Natural Sugar as a sweetener, but feel free to use any sweetening you like. Florida Crystals can be found in health food stores and most better grocery stores.

Plain Super Soymilk

In soymilk lingo "plain" means without vanilla flavoring. Plain soymilk is sweet and flavorful, there's just no vanilla added. We really don't think our plain super soymilk is plain at all but we have to go along with the terminology that's already out there in the industry.

2 cups water
2 tablespoons Florida Crystals Natural Sugar
  (or other sugar)
2/3 cup (2 scoops) **Whole Nectar® Ultimate Soy Protein Smoothie Mix**

Makes 18 oz.

Place all ingredients in the Vita-Mix container in order listed. Secure the lid. Select Variable #1, turn to ON, and quickly increase speed to #10. Run about 20 seconds until smooth. Decrease speed back down to Variable #3 and run about 10 seconds. Turn to OFF. Refrigerate and serve well-chilled. Shake well before serving.

149 calories per 8 oz serving: 14 g protein, 1 g fat, 21 g carbohydrate; 71 mg sodium; 0 mg cholesterol.

To Make Very Lightly Sweetened Version: Leave out the sugar.

Nectar Note: Whole Nectar Super Soymilk can be used in cooking and makes great hot drinks. In addition, soymilk can be used in place of dairy in many recipes. Soymilk is sweeter than cow's milk, however, so adjust your recipe to allow for that difference.

Chocolate Super Soymilk

Making really good chocolate soymilk is actually a no-brainer. Just add a quality powdered chocolate (like Ghirardelli®) to our soy smoothie mix. It's that easy. We think you'll be impressed with the taste and the fact that an 8 oz. glass has 15 grams of protein - pretty impressive for a glass of chocolate milk and three times the protein of the same amount of Chocolate Silk®.

2 cups water
5 tablespoons Ghirardelli® Sweet Ground Chocolate
2/3 cup (2 scoops) **Whole Nectar® Ultimate Soy**
    Protein Smoothie Mix

Makes 18 oz.

Place all ingredients in the Vita-Mix container in order listed. Secure the lid. Select Variable #1, turn to ON, and quickly increase speed to #10. Run about 20 seconds until smooth. Decrease speed back down to Variable #3 and run about 10 seconds. Turn to OFF. Refrigerate and serve well-chilled. Shake well before serving.

173 calories per 8 oz serving: 15 g protein, 2 g fat, 25 g carbohydrate; 71 mg sodium; 0 mg cholesterol.

Nectar Note: Our Chocolate Super Soymilk can be stored in the refrigerator for up to 5 days. Like all soymilks, shake well before serving. And it makes great hot chocolate. Just heat gently and serve. **Ghirardelli® Sweet Ground Chocolate** can be found in most large grocery stores. It's usually in the baking chocolate section rather than the powdered chocolate drink section. Grocery stores can be tricky that way.

Strawberry Super Soymilk

Fill in those gaps between meals with this fruity, protein powered, low calorie snack. Serve immediately and enjoy!

1 cup water
1 scoop (5 tablespoons) **Whole Nectar® Ultimate Soy**
   Protein Smoothie Mix
1 tablespoon Florida Crystals Natural Sugar
   (or other sugar)
1/2 cup frozen, unsweetened strawberries
1/2 cup ice

Makes 16 oz.

Place all ingredients in the Vita-Mix container in order listed. Secure the lid. Select Variable #1, turn to ON, and quickly increase speed to #10. Switch to High. Run about 20 seconds until smooth. Serve immediately.

97 calories per 8 oz serving: 8 g protein, 1 g fat, 15 g carbohydrate; 46 mg sodium; 0 mg cholesterol.

Peach Super Soymilk

Fruit flavored super soymilks are light and refreshing. Make them icy cold and serve immediately.

1 cup water
1 scoop (5 tablespoons) **Whole Nectar® Ultimate Soy Protein Smoothie Mix**
1 tablespoon Florida Crystals Natural Sugar
   (or other sugar)
1/2 cup frozen, unsweetened peach slices
1/2 cup ice

Makes 16 oz.

Place all ingredients in the Vita-Mix container in order listed. Secure the lid. Select Variable #1, turn to ON, and quickly increase speed to #10. Switch to High. Run about 20 seconds until smooth. Serve immediately.

99 calories per 8 oz serving: 8 g protein, 1 g fat, 15 g carbohydrate; 40 mg sodium; 0 mg cholesterol.

Berry Super Soymilk

Using our fruit flavored super soymilk recipe template you can create your own custom blends. Just replace the frozen berries in this recipe with an equal amount of any unsweetened, frozen fruit of your choice.

1 cup water
1 scoop (5 tablespoons) **Whole Nectar® Ultimate Soy Protein Smoothie Mix**
1 tablespoon Florida Crystals Natural Sugar
(or other sugar)
1/2 cup frozen mixed raspberries and blackberries
(unsweetened)
1/2 cup ice

Makes 16 oz.

Place all ingredients in the Vita-Mix container in order listed. Secure the lid. Select Variable #1, turn to ON, and quickly increase speed to #10. Switch to High. Run about 20 seconds until smooth. Serve immediately

112 calories per 8 oz serving: 8 g protein, 1 g fat, 19 g carbohydrate; 40 mg sodium; 0 mg cholesterol.

Vanilla Almond Super Soymilk

Get nuts! Then make this. Rich, creamy and nutty, it's good all by itself. Just chill, shake and serve. Or use it to blend up one of our favorite "half&half" drinks - half almond soymilk and half orange juice or half almond soymilk and half cherry yogurt (highly recommended). This blend is a great base for all kinds shakes and smoothies and will store well in the refrigerator for up to five days.

2 cups water
2 teaspoons pure vanilla extract
2 tablespoons Florida Crystals Natural Sugar
(or other sugar)
1/2 cup raw almonds

2/3 cup (2 scoops) **Whole Nectar® Ultimate Soy Protein Smoothie Mix**
Makes 22 oz.

Place all ingredients, *except smoothie mix*, in the Vita-Mix container. Secure the lid. Select Variable #1, turn to ON, and quickly increase speed to #10. Switch to HIGH. Run about 30 seconds until almonds are smooth. Turn to Off. Add smoothie mix. Select Variable #1, turn to ON, and quickly increase speed to #10. Run about 20 seconds until smooth. Refrigerate and serve well-chilled. Shake well before serving.

271 calories per 8 oz serving: 17 g protein, 14 g fat, 21 g carbohydrate; 58 mg sodium; 0 mg cholesterol.

Variations:
Vanilla Multi-Nut Super Soymilk - Reduce almonds to 1/4 cup. Add 2 tablespoons walnuts and 2 tablespoons pistachios (or cashews). **Hot Drink -** Add a sprinkle of cinnamon and/or nutmeg and heat gently. **Almond Chocolate Malt -** Blend 1 cup almond soymilk, 1 tablespoon powdered chocolate, 1 tablespoon chocolate malt and 1/2 cup ice.

Multi-Grain Super Soymilk

If you're making an effort to eat more whole grain foods, don't forget about smoothies. Whip up our multi-grain blend and store in the refrigerator, ready for use in drinks and smoothies. We have quite a collection of "half&half" drinks using Multi-Grain Super Soymilk. Try some of our favorites shown below.

2 cups water
2 tablespoons Florida Crystals Natural Sugar
    (or other sugar)
2 tablespoons rolled oats (no cooking-use right out of the box)
2 tablespoons cooked brown rice
2/3 cup (2 scoops) **Whole Nectar® Ultimate Soy**
    Protein Smoothie Mix

Makes 20 oz.

Place all ingredients in the Vita-Mix container in order listed. Secure the lid. Select Variable #1, turn to ON, and quickly increase speed to #10. Switch to HIGH. Run about 20 seconds until smooth. Decrease speed back down to Variable #3 and run about 10 seconds. Turn to OFF. Refrigerate and serve well-chilled. Shake well before serving.

160 calories per 8 oz serving: 14 g protein, 1 g fat, 24 g carbohydrate; 64 mg sodium; 0 mg cholesterol.

Variations: Blend half Multi-Grain Super Soymilk and half apple juice. Or half Multi-Grain Super Soymilk and half tropical peach yogurt. Or blend 1/2 cup Multi-Grain Super Soymilk, 1/2 banana and 1/2 cup frozen berries.

Java Banana Chocolate Shake

Add banana and coffee to our creamy Chocolate Super Soymilk and you have a mid-morning snack that's hard to beat.

1 cup Whole Nectar® Chocolate Super Soymilk
   (see page 95 for recipe)
1/2 tablespoon coffee crystals
1 teaspoon pure vanilla extract
1/2 banana
1 cup ice

Makes about 16 oz.

Place all ingredients in the Vita-Mix container in order listed. Secure the lid.   Select Variable #1, turn to ON, and quickly increase speed to #10.   Switch to HIGH.   Run about 20 seconds until smooth. Use tamper, if necessary, to help circulate ingredients.

113 calories per 8 oz serving: 8 g protein, 1 g fat, 19 g carbohydrate; 36 mg sodium; 0 mg cholesterol

Power Coffee Shake

Don't just have a latte, power it up with Whole Nectar. Great taste and healthy soy protein will keep you humming right along.

1 cup Whole Nectar® Plain Super Soymilk
1 cup strong brewed coffee (chilled)
2 tablespoons Florida Crystals Natural Sugar
   (or other sugar)
1 to 1-1/4 cups ice

Makes about 20 oz.

Place all ingredients in the Vita-Mix container in order listed. Secure the lid. Select Variable #1, turn to ON, and quickly increase speed to #10. Switch to HIGH. Run about 20 seconds until smooth. Use tamper, if necessary, to help circulate ingredients.

123 calories per 10 oz serving: 7 g protein, 0 g fat, 23 g carbohydrate; 36 mg sodium; 0 mg cholesterol

Nectar Note: The classic latte is usually made from coffee brewed from beans with an "intense" flavor like espresso. That same distinct flavor also makes a great shake.
Variations: Instead of brewed coffee, use 1 cup water and 1 to 2 tablespoons coffee crystals.
Vanilla Coffee Shake - Add 1 teaspoon vanilla extract to above recipe or use vanilla soymilk instead of plain.

Chai Peach Shake

If you think tea is for wimps, then you haven't tried chai. Chai is bold, sweet and spicy. Blend chai and peaches and the result is a shake that will remind you of the best peach pie you've ever had!

1 cup chai liquid concentrate (undiluted)
1/2 cup water
1 scoop (5 tablespoons) **Whole Nectar® Ultimate Soy Protein Smoothie Mix**
1 cup frozen peach slices (unsweetened)

Makes about 22 oz.

Place all ingredients in the Vita-Mix container in order listed. Secure the lid. Select Variable #1, turn to ON, and quickly increase speed to #10. Switch to HIGH. Run about 20 seconds until smooth. Use tamper, if necessary, to help circulate ingredients.

168 calories per 11oz serving: 9 g protein, 1 g fat, 31 g carbohydrate; 48 mg sodium; 0 mg cholesterol

Nectar Note: Making chai from scratch is fun and will make your whole house smell wonderful. But it's quite a project. Fortunately there's a short cut. Look for the chai liquid concentrates in 32 oz. packages at large grocery stores or health food stores.

Ginger Tea Shake

Sweet, fresh ginger and the unique flavor of green tea make a very stimulating blend. This is our version of a drink that's a favorite in many Asian cultures. If you're having a midmorning energy crisis, we highly recommend this shake instead of the usual cup of coffee. If you're not a fan of green tea, use black instead. Whether you use black or green, don't be afraid to be brew it strong. That's how you end up with a flavorful shake.

3/4 cup Whole Nectar® Vanilla Super Soymilk
3/4 cup double strength green tea (unsweetened, chilled)
1-1/2 tablespoons Florida Crystals Natural Sugar
   (or other sugar)
1 quarter-sized piece fresh ginger (peeled)
1 to 1-1/4 cups ice

Makes about 16 oz.

Place all ingredients in the Vita-Mix container in order listed. Secure the lid. Select Variable #1, turn to ON, and quickly increase speed to #10. Switch to HIGH. Run about 20 seconds until smooth. Use tamper, if necessary, to help circulate ingredients.

92 calories per 8 oz serving: 5 g protein, 1 g fat, 17 g carbohydrate; 27 mg sodium; 0 mg cholesterol

Nutrition Highlights: Both black and green tea (but not herb tea) contain flavonoids that may have as much antioxidant power as those in fruits and vegetables. In addition, some studies suggest that regular tea drinkers have greater bone density and are less likely to develop osteoporosis.
Variations: Try it as a hot drink. Just leave out the ice, blend and heat gently.

Mexican Coffee Shake

We have the Mexican culture to thank for the chocolate drink. The Aztecs drank prodigious amounts of a blend of ground cacao beans and water because they believed it was important for their health. Over time the Aztec drink evolved with the addition of sweetening, vanilla and cinnamon. We use tasty vanilla super soymilk in our representation of this delicious blend.

1 cup Whole Nectar® Vanilla Super Soymilk
1/2 teaspoon pure vanilla extract
1/2 to 1 tablespoon coffee crystals
1 tablespoon Ghirardelli® Sweet Ground Chocolate
1 sprinkle of cinnamon
1/2 to 3/4 cups ice

Makes about 12 oz.

Place all ingredients in the Vita-Mix container in order listed. Secure the lid. Select Variable #1, turn to ON, and quickly increase speed to #10. Switch to HIGH. Run about 20 seconds until smooth. Use tamper, if necessary, to help circulate ingredients.

90 calories per 6 oz serving: 7 g protein, 1 g fat, 14 g carbohydrate; 36 mg sodium; 0 mg cholesterol

Nutrition Highlights: The Aztecs may have been right about their health drink. Both chocolate and coffee have antioxidants (polyphenols) with healthful properties similar to those in tea.
Variations: Add 1 tablespoon sweetened coconut flakes and/or 1 or 2 tablespoons of almonds.

Chai Apple Smoothie

If you haven't tried chai, you're missing out on one of the seven wonders of the drink world. Chai smoothies are one of our favorite ways to enjoy this spicy tea latte. By the way, our chai-apple blend has a wonderful apple pie flavor.

1 cup Oregon Chai® Kashmir Green Tea concentrate
(undiluted)
1 scoop (5 tablespoons) **Whole Nectar® Ultimate Soy Protein Smoothie Mix**
1/2 apple
1-1/2 to 2 cups ice

Makes about 20 oz.

Place all ingredients in the Vita-Mix container in order listed. Secure the lid. Select Variable #1, turn to ON, and quickly increase speed to #10. Switch to HIGH. Run about 20 seconds until smooth. Use tamper, if necessary, to help circulate ingredients.

167 calories per 10 oz serving: 8 g protein, 1 g fat, 31 g carbohydrate; 91 mg sodium; 0 mg cholesterol.

Nutrition Highlights: Green tea is on every health expert's super food list. It has powerful antioxidants that may be more potent than vitamin C or E.

Coffee Almond Smoothie

If you typically start the day with coffee and a bagel, why not "bump it up" with this power iced cappuccino. Almonds, oats and lots of protein put this blend on a whole new level for iced coffee.

3/4 cup vanilla almond milk
1 teaspoon pure vanilla extract
1/8 teaspoon almond extract
2 tablespoons honey
1 scoop (5 tablespoons) **Whole Nectar® Ultimate Soy**
   Protein Smoothie Mix
1/2 - 1 tablespoon coffee crystals
1/3 cup oatmeal (right out of box-no need to cook)
5 almonds
1-1/2 to 2 cups ice

Makes about 20 oz.

Place all ingredients in the Vita-Mix container in order listed. Secure the lid. Select Variable #1, turn to ON, and quickly increase speed to #10. Switch to HIGH. Run about 20 seconds until smooth. Use tamper, if necessary, to help circulate ingredients.

230 calories per 10 oz serving: 10 g protein, 4 g fat, 39 g carbohydrate; 79 mg sodium; 0 mg cholesterol.

Nutrition Highlights: If you like coffee, the good news is no valid study has ever associated any negative health effects with moderate coffee drinking. In fact, the latest research suggests that coffee may have healthy antioxidant compounds similar, but possibly even greater, than tea.

Chai Berry Melon Smoothie

The bold, spicy flavor of chai adds a whole new dimension to the berry smoothie. Chai is an ancient beverage from India that is typically a mixture of black tea, ginger, cardamom, cinnamon, cloves and other spices that vary by region and culture. Lightly tart berries are a wonderful contrast for the sweet, complex spiciness of chai.

1 cup chai liquid concentrate (undiluted)
1 scoop (5 tablespoons) **Whole Nectar® Ultimate Soy Protein Smoothie Mix**
1/2 cup frozen honeydew or cantaloupe cubes
1 cup frozen blackberries or blueberries (unsweetened)

Makes about 16 oz.

Place all ingredients in the Vita-Mix container in order listed. Secure the lid. Select Variable #1, turn to ON, and quickly increase speed to #10. Switch to HIGH. Run about 20 seconds until smooth. Use tamper, if necessary, to help circulate ingredients.

201 calories per 8 oz serving: 9 g protein, 1 g fat, 40 g carbohydrate; 53 mg sodium; 0 mg cholesterol

Nutrition Highlights: Most nutritious foods have one or more of the following characteristics: rich color, strong flavor, or distinctive smell. It was no surprise, then, when researchers confirmed what we had suspected all along - the same compounds that cause our favorite spices to have such intense flavors and smells are also powerful antioxidants with many health properties.

Java Chocolate Chip Smoothie

This smoothie sounds really decadent but it has only 200 calories in 10 oz. A few chocolate chips can go a long way when you use them the way we do in this recipe.

1 cup water
1 scoop (5 tablespoons) **Whole Nectar® Ultimate Soy Protein Smoothie Mix**
1-1/2 tablespoons coffee crystals
2-1/2 tablespoons Florida Crystals Natural Sugar
   (or other sugar)
2 to 2-1/4 cups ice

2 tablespoons milk chocolate chips

Makes about 20 oz.

Place all ingredients, *except chocolate chips*, in the Vita-Mix container in order listed. Secure the lid. Select Variable #1, turn to ON, and quickly increase speed to #10. Switch to HIGH. Run about 20 seconds until smooth. Use tamper, if necessary, to help circulate ingredients. Stop machine, add chips and process on Variable #10 about 20 seconds until chips become flecks.

200 calories per 10 oz serving: 8 g protein, 5 g fat, 30 g carbohydrate; 40 mg sodium; 4 mg cholesterol

Variations: For a richer smoothie use milk or half & half instead of water.

Nectar Note: Florida Crystals brand sugar has a very good taste and is available in most better supermarkets and health food stores. Feel free to substitute any other sugar or sweetening in it's place.

Chocolate Strawberry Shake

Strawberries add wonderful fruit flavor to this delicious, low calorie chocolate shake.

1 cup Whole Nectar® Chocolate Super Soymilk
(see page 95 for recipe)
1/2 cup strawberries
1 cup ice

Makes about 16 oz.

Place all ingredients in the Vita-Mix container in order listed. Secure the lid. Select Variable #1, turn to ON, and quickly increase speed to #10. Switch to HIGH. Run about 20 seconds until smooth. Use tamper, if necessary, to help circulate ingredients.

100 calories per 8 oz serving: 8 g protein, 1 g fat, 16 g carbohydrate; 42 mg sodium; 0 mg cholesterol

Cinnamon Peanut Butter Shake

If you like peanut butter, you haven't lived until you blend it up with a little cinnamon. Peanut butter is a very healthy food if you buy the kind that's "just peanuts". Or, make your own. You can do it with a Vita-Mix.

1-1/2 cups Whole Nectar® Vanilla Super Soymilk
   (see page 93 for recipe)
2 tablespoons peanut butter
2 tablespoons Whole Nectar® Ultimate Soy
   Protein Smoothie Mix
1/8 teaspoon cinnamon
1 to 1-1/4 cups ice

Makes about 20 oz.

Place all ingredients in the Vita-Mix container in order listed. Secure the lid. Select Variable #1, turn to ON, and quickly increase speed to #10. Switch to HIGH. Run about 20 seconds until smooth. Use tamper, if necessary, to help circulate ingredients.

236 calories per 10 oz serving: 18 g protein, 8 g fat, 21 g carbohydrate; 69 mg sodium; 0 mg cholesterol

Nutrition Highlights: Peanuts are high in fiber and have more protein than any other nuts.

Variations: Add 1 teaspoon toasted wheat germ *or* add 1 tablespoon coffee crystals (yes, coffee and peanut butter are really good together) *or* add 1/2 banana.

Power Frostee

If you like Wendy's Frosty, may we recommend a Whole Nectar Power Frostee instead? Our Power Frostee has almost twice the protein, less calories, less fat and we think it tastes great, too.

1 cup nonfat milk
1 scoop (5 tablespoons) **Whole Nectar® Ultimate Soy Protein Smoothie Mix**
3 tablespoons Ghirardelli® sweet ground chocolate
1 tablespoon Carnation® chocolate malted milk
2 to 2-1/4 cups ice

Makes about 20 oz.

Place all ingredients in the Vita-Mix container in order listed. Secure the lid. Select Variable #1, turn to ON, and quickly increase speed to #10. Switch to HIGH. Run about 20 seconds until smooth. Use tamper, if necessary, to help circulate ingredients.

160 calories per 10 oz serving: 13 g protein, 1 g fat, 25 g carbohydrate; 109 mg sodium; 2 mg cholesterol.

Nutrition Highlights: Here's the profile on a Wendy's Frosty per 10 oz. serving: 275 calories, 7 g protein, 7 g fat, 47 g carbohydrate; 167 mg sodium; 30 mg cholesterol.

Nectar Note: Ghirardelli® brand powdered chocolate is a great tasting, quality chocolate that's worth hunting down in your local supermarket. A decent substitute is Hershey's® chocolate milk mix but it doesn't have near the chocolate flavor so you'll need to use more.

Chocolate Almond Banana Smoothie

We've enjoyed the Odwalla® Future Shake so much, we just had to come up with something similar. This is our taste-alike version in the form of a smoothie.

1 cup water
1 scoop (5 tablespoons) **Whole Nectar® Ultimate Soy Protein Smoothie Mix**
2 tablespoons Hershey's® Chocolate Milk Mix
1/3 cup oatmeal (right out of box-no need to cook)
5 almonds
1 frozen banana (broken in thirds)
1 to 1-1/2 cups ice

Makes about 20 oz.

Place all ingredients in the Vita-Mix container in order listed. Secure the lid. Select Variable #1, turn to ON, and quickly increase speed to #10. Switch to HIGH. Run about 20 seconds until smooth. Use tamper, if necessary, to help circulate ingredients.

215 calories per 10 oz serving: 10 g protein, 4 g fat, 37 g carbohydrate; 80 mg sodium; 0 mg cholesterol.

Nutrition Highlights: For a number of years, almonds were lumped in with potato chips in the "high fat snack to be avoided" food group. Now we know better. Almonds contain beneficial unsaturated fats and other important nutrients. They can certainly be considered part of a healthy diet if eaten in moderation.

Chocolate Orange Smoothie

This tasty chocolate treat is protein powered and rich in vitamin C.

1/2 cup orange frozen juice concentrate
1/3 cup water
1 scoop (5 tablespoons) **Whole Nectar® Ultimate Soy Protein Smoothie Mix**
4 tablespoons Hershey's® Chocolate Milk Mix
1 orange (peeled and halved)
1-1/4 to 1-3/4 cups ice

Makes about 20 oz.

Place all ingredients in the Vita-Mix container in order listed. Secure the lid. Select Variable #1, turn to ON, and quickly increase speed to #10. Switch to HIGH. Run about 20 seconds until smooth. Use tamper, if necessary, to help circulate ingredients.

268 calories per 10 oz serving: 8 g protein, 1 g fat, 56 g carbohydrate; 71 mg sodium; 0 mg cholesterol.

Nutrition Highlights: Citrus fruit is so nutritious, you really should try to have some every day. This smoothie is a way to have your chocolate and citrus too.

Banana Almond Smoothie

If you're in the mood for something simple, creamy and delicious, this smoothie is it. And, good news - almonds are healthy and come highly recommended by the health experts. They're high in fat, however, so you have to have some self-control. Since almost no one can snack on just a few almonds, putting a few in a smoothie is a good way to practice moderation.

3/4 cup nonfat milk
1 tablespoon honey
1 teaspoon pure vanilla extract
1/8 teaspoon almond extract (optional)
1 scoop (5 tablespoons) **Whole Nectar® Ultimate Soy**
    Protein Smoothie Mix
1-1/2 frozen bananas (broken in thirds)
10 almonds
3/4 to 1-1/4 cups ice

Makes about 20 oz.

Place all ingredients in the Vita-Mix container in order listed. Secure the lid. Select Variable #1, turn to ON, and quickly increase speed to #10. Switch to HIGH. Run about 20 seconds until smooth. Use tamper, if necessary, to help circulate ingredients.

240 calories per 10 oz serving: 12 g protein, 4 g fat, 41 g carbohydrate; 89 mg sodium; 2 mg cholesterol.

Nutrition Highlights: Bananas are the leading fruit source of potassium, a mineral that is vital for controlling the body's fluid balance. Almonds are rich in calcium, vitamin E and fiber.

Peanut Butter Banana Smoothie

Attention peanut butter banana lovers! Believe it or not, you can have your favorite food and not have to throw your low fat lifestyle out the window. A 10 ounce serving of this smoothie has only 6 grams of fat and loads of flavor.

3/4 cup nonfat milk
1 teaspoon honey
1 scoop (5 tablespoons) **Whole Nectar® Ultimate Soy Protein Smoothie Mix**
1-1/2 tablespoons peanut butter
1 banana
1-1/4 to 1-3/4 cups ice

Makes about 20 oz.

Place all ingredients in the Vita-Mix container in order listed. Secure the lid. Select Variable #1, turn to ON, and quickly increase speed to #10. Switch to HIGH. Run about 20 seconds until smooth. Use tamper, if necessary, to help circulate ingredients.

234 calories per 10 oz serving: 14 g protein, 6 g fat, 30 g carbohydrate; 88 mg sodium; 2 mg cholesterol.

Nutrition Highlights: Peanut butter is a very nutritious food - just be careful what kind you buy. Read the label and make sure it's just peanuts. Don't buy cheap commercial peanut butter. It's usually a scary mixture of third rate peanuts, hydrogenated oils (trans fat) and sugar. Better yet, make your own. If you have a Vita-Mix it's easy and fun. And the taste of fresh ground peanut butter can't be beat. **Nectar Note:** A tablespoon of toasted wheat germ is a great addition to this smoothie.

Banana Sunflower Malt Smoothie

Power up a vanilla malt with sunflower seeds and banana. You may find this smoothie hard to beat as an afternoon snack.

3/4 cup vanilla rice milk
2 tablespoons Carnation® Malted Milk Original
1 scoop (5 tablespoons) **Whole Nectar® Ultimate Soy Protein Smoothie Mix**
1 tablespoon raw sunflower seeds
1 frozen banana (broken in thirds)
3/4 to 1-1/4 cups ice

Makes about 20 oz.

Place all ingredients in the Vita-Mix container in order listed. Secure the lid. Select Variable #1, turn to ON, and quickly increase speed to #10. Switch to HIGH. Run about 20 seconds until smooth. Use tamper, if necessary, to help circulate ingredients.

206 calories per 10 oz serving: 11 g protein, 4 g fat, 33 g carbohydrate; 97 mg sodium; 2 mg cholesterol.

Nutrition Highlights: Sunflower seeds will give your smoothie a bump in vitamin E, thiamin, magnesium, iron, and zinc.

Peanut Butter & Jelly Smoothie

The peanut butter and jelly sandwich connoisseurs in your house might want to give this sweet treat a whirl.

3/4 cup Whole Nectar® Vanilla Super Soymilk
(see page 93 for recipe)
2 tablespoons Whole Nectar® Ultimate Soy Protein Smoothie Mix
2 tablespoons peanut butter
(or 3-4 tablespoons roasted, shelled peanuts)
1 teaspoon strawberry preserves
1/2 cup frozen strawberries (unsweetened)
1 to 1-1/4 cups ice

Makes about 16 oz.

Place all ingredients in the Vita-Mix container in order listed. Secure the lid. Select Variable #1, turn to ON, and quickly increase speed to #10. Switch to HIGH. Run about 20 seconds until smooth. Use tamper, if necessary, to help circulate ingredients.

201 calories per 8 oz serving: 13 g protein, 7 g fat, 19 g carbohydrate; 49 mg sodium; 0 mg cholesterol.

Variations: Other preserves and frozen fruit (such as raspberry preserves and frozen raspberries) can be substituted for the strawberry preserves and the strawberries in this recipe.

Creamy Vanilla Almond Smoothie

It's a festive nog and a smoothie all in one. Don't wait for the holidays to try this treat.

1/2 cup Whole Nectar® Vanilla Almond Soymilk
(see page 99 for recipe)
1/2 cup tapioca pudding
1 tablespoon Whole Nectar® Ultimate Soy
Protein Smoothie Mix
1 sprinkle of nutmeg and/or cinnamon
1/2 to 3/4 cup ice

Makes about 12 oz.

Place all ingredients in the Vita-Mix container in order listed. Secure the lid. Select Variable #1, turn to ON, and quickly increase speed to #10. Switch to HIGH. Run about 20 seconds until smooth. Use tamper, if necessary, to help circulate ingredients.

174 calories per 6 oz serving: 9 g protein, 7 g fat, 19 g carbohydrate; 166 mg sodium; 62 mg cholesterol

Variations: Add 1/2 banana. Or use vanilla soymilk instead of almond soymilk.

Chocolate Banana Brownie Smoothie

Yes, you can have a snack that has both rich chocolate taste and a passing grade on the nutrition scorecard. The key is moderation. No valid scientific study has ever found anything unhealthful about chocolate. But it is high fat, and like all high fat foods you need to show good judgment.

3/4 cup nonfat milk
1 teaspoon pure vanilla extract
1 scoop (5 tablespoons) **Whole Nectar® Ultimate Soy Protein Smoothie Mix**
3 tablespoons Ghirardelli® sweet ground chocolate
1 medium banana
2 to 2-1/4 cups ice

chopped walnuts
Makes about 20 oz.

Place all ingredients, *except walnuts*, in the Vita-Mix container in order listed. Secure the lid. Select Variable #1, turn to ON, and quickly increase speed to #10. Switch to HIGH. Run about 20 seconds until smooth. Use tamper, if necessary, to help circulate ingredients. Make smoothie thick enough to eat with a spoon. Serve in a glass topped with chopped walnuts.

188 calories per 10 oz serving: 12 g protein, 2 g fat, 34 g carbohydrate; 87 mg sodium; 2 mg cholesterol (without walnuts)

Variations:
New Mexican Brownie: Use toasted pinion nuts instead of walnuts.
Rocky Road: Top with mini-marshmallows along with the walnuts.
Java Brownie: Add 1 tablespoon coffee crystals.
For a richer smoothie: Use whole milk instead of nonfat milk.
Nectar Note: Use a quality powdered chocolate like Ghirardelli® in your smoothie, and you'll need less chocolate to get great flavor.

Southwest Banana Nut Shake

Who would think of putting pinions in a blender? We did and found out that their unique, mildly creamy flavor is delicious with banana. Try it. We think you'll love the subtle flavor in this shake as much as we do.

3/4 cup vanilla oat milk
3 tablespoons Whole Nectar® Ultimate Soy
  Protein Smoothie Mix
1 medium banana
2 tablespoons raw pinion nuts
1 teaspoon raw pumpkin seeds
1 cup ice

Makes about 16 oz.

Place all ingredients in the Vita-Mix container in order listed. Secure the lid. Select Variable #1, turn to ON, and quickly increase speed to #10. Switch to HIGH. Run about 20 seconds until smooth. Use tamper, if necessary, to help circulate ingredients.

182 calories per 8 oz serving:8 g protein, 5 g fat, 27 g carbohydrate; 66 mg sodium; 0 mg cholesterol

Nutrition Highlights: Pinion nuts (also called pine nuts by Eastern city people) are rich in thiamine, iron and magnesium. Pumpkins seeds are also rich in iron.
Nectar Note: Raw pinion nuts and raw pumpkin seeds are dried but not roasted and salted. Because they have no added oil or salt, they're ideal for smoothies. Raw nuts and seeds can be found in larger health food markets and should be stored in the refrigerator.

Vanilla Super Malt

Our protein packed super malt is rich in sweet, vanilla flavor but
very low calorie.

1 cup water
1 scoop (5 tablespoons) **Whole Nectar® Ultimate Soy**
  Protein Smoothie Mix
1 tablespoon Florida Crystals Natural Sugar
  (or other sugar)
1 tablespoon Carnation® Malted Milk Original
1/2 teaspoon pure vanilla extract
1 cup ice

Makes about 16 oz.

Place all ingredients in the Vita-Mix container in order listed.
Secure the lid. Select Variable #1, turn to ON, and quickly increase
speed to #10. Switch to HIGH. Run about 20 seconds until smooth.
Use tamper, if necessary, to help circulate ingredients.

*99 calories per 8 oz serving: 9 g protein, 1 g fat, 15 g carbohydrate; 54 mg
sodium; 1 mg cholesterol*

Variation:
  Vanilla Orange Super Malt: Use orange juice instead of water
  and increase vanilla to 1 teaspoon.

"Poor eating habits are like cigarette smoking: Their ill effects may not become evident for many years, but they can damage your health. You can eat a high-cholesterol diet for a long time without feeling your arteries slamming shut. Consequently, many people put off seeking good nutrition until their health is compromised. Ironically, the benefits of healthy eating are usually noticed rather quickly, usually in terms of more energy. (This is especially the case for meal skippers.)"

Evelyn Tribole, MS RD
from her book *"Eating on the Run"*

Smoothie Clinic

Okay, so you followed the recipe (or thought you did) and your smoothie didn't quite come out the way you expected. The good news is that it's often possible to "repair" a smoothie that's already made. Or, at the very least, give you a tip for next time. Here are some fixes to try:

Too sweet? What do you do? Throw it out and start over? No way! You can repair it by:

Adding more ice or adding a little water (1/4 cup) and ice.

Or add fresh lemon juice, 1 teaspoon at a time, until you have it the way you want it. This is our favorite unsweetening method for most fruit smoothies because it doesn't dilute the flavors like adding water and ice will.

Or add a little more milk if it's a milk based smoothie like *Peanut Butter Banana*. You'll probably also have to add more ice when you do this.

Or add a little plain yogurt. It's very tart and as little as a tablespoon will offset the sweet. If you like a tart taste in smoothies, consider replacing the vanilla or fruit flavored yogurt in recipes with plain. Using very ripe fruit (especially bananas) will increase the sweetness of a smoothie. If your fruit is very ripe, you may want to use less than you usually do if you don't like your smoothies very sweet.

Not sweet enough? I guess the answer is pretty obvious, but we'll give it anyway:

Add either more frozen juice concentrate (whatever kind is in the recipe), honey or Florida Crystals. It doesn't take much. As little as 1 teaspoon in a 20 oz. smoothie will really increase the sweetness.

Too thick and icy?

With the machine off, add water, milk or any liquid compatible with the ingredients in your smoothie, about 1/4 cup at a time, stir a little with the tamper, and run until smooth (about 20 seconds). The more you run the machine, the thinner it will get.

Or, let the container of smoothie ingredients sit on your kitchen counter for a few minutes. When the frozen ingredients thaw out a bit, stir and process again for about 20 seconds.

Not thick enough?

With the machine off, add ice (about 1/2 cup at a time). Turn on and run about 15 seconds. If it's still not thick enough, stop the machine and add more ice. Don't over process. Running the machine longer doesn't make it thicker. In fact, just the opposite is true. If you're following recipes and all your smoothies are coming out watery, you may be running the machine too long. About 20 seconds on High is all the processing you need for most smoothies made in the Vita-Mix.

Is the consistency too creamy or not creamy enough for your taste?

A lot of banana, yogurt or frozen fruit in a recipe tends to result in a creamier texture. When you make a smoothie with frozen fruit, you'll need less ice than making the same recipe with fresh fruit. And the resulting smoothie will have a creamier texture. It's personal preference. You can make them either way and decide which one is for you.

More Tips For The Smoothie Mixologist

Fresh fruit and frozen fruit are interchangeable in recipes. You'll need to make an adjustment, however, for the balance of frozen and unfrozen ingredients. For instance, if the smoothie recipe calls for frozen fruit and you're using fresh fruit instead, you'll need to increase the amount of ice over what we recommend in the recipe. The reverse is true if you're using frozen fruit in a recipe written for fresh fruit.

More about ice. Our smoothie recipes suggest an amount of ice that's geared to produce a fairly thick blend. But ice has variability (depending upon the temperature of your freezer) so you may end up using slightly more or less than the amount we've suggested in the recipe. The recipes were written for cups of icemaker style ice. If you're using ice cube tray ice, the equivalent is 6 large ice cubes for every cup of ice in the recipe.

More is not necessarily better. No matter how much you love strawberries, for instance, we would not recommend doubling the amount of strawberries over what we suggest in a recipe. The perfect power smoothie is a balance of frozen and unfrozen ingredients. More strawberries won't necessarily give you more flavor because you'll have to add more ice to compensate.

To boost or not to boost? Let's face it. There are some pretty far out things people add to their smoothies. Many of them are promoted by the modern version of the snake oil salesman. Most are expensive, some are of dubious nutritional value and almost all will seriously detract from the taste of the smoothie. Some real food boosters we can recommend are toasted wheat germ, flax seed, oat bran, wheat bran, and sunflower seeds. All are very nutritious additions that won't affect the flavor much if used in small amounts. Start with amounts like 1/2 teaspoon to see if you like the taste.

9 Ways Power Smoothies Can Be The Centerpiece Of A Lean & Healthy Lifestyle

1. Help You Avoid The Perils Of Meal Skipping

Skipping meals may not sound that bad on the face of it. Or it might actually sound like a good thing (skip a meal-lose some weight).   In fact, this habit can take an enormous toll on your health and pack on the pounds. Here's why:

You Can't Trust the Judgment of a Starving Person

There's solid evidence that people who skip meals are much more likely to be overweight. Why? Because they usually end up eating a lot more food and make poor food choices compared to folks who eat 3 reasonable meals spread out through the day.

This is particularly true when breakfast is the missed meal. Breakfast dodgers, in fact, are notorious for an eating pattern we call "avalanche eating". Avalanche eaters start the day small - little or no breakfast and an insignificant lunch. By mid-afternoon they're starved and the eating just gets bigger and bigger - and then roars out of control taking everything in it's path! Hey. What can I say. A starving person just can't be expected to be particularly discriminating about what and how much they eat.

Miss Meals - Get Fat

Most people know that their body burns calories

according to their level of activity. But many don't know that their metabolic rate is also significantly affected by starving. Even one skipped meal can cause the body to go on starvation red alert. Lack of food causes the brain to trigger a slow down of metabolism and an increase in fat storage.

Why is missing breakfast especially bad? Think about it this way. When you get up in the morning, you've actually already fasted for at least 8 hours while you slept. Postponing the first meal of the day is sure to set off the starvation alarm to save fuel and store fat.

No Food = Crash and Burn

Yet another casualty of meal skipping is your energy level. Missed meals cause your blood sugar to plummet. The result: lack of energy, drowsiness and just a general lack of motivation. Even your brain is affected by lack of food. So much so, that breakfast eaters, both young and old, routinely outscore breakfast dodgers in tests designed to measure alertness and problem solving ability.

A Smoothie Fits Perfectly
In Those Meal Gaps

Skipping meals is not something to be taken lightly. It's a habit that is highly likely to aid and abet any inclination you may already have to overeat, gain unwanted pounds, and make poor food choices. Power smoothies will come to your rescue. We're not suggesting all your meals come out of a blender. We are suggesting that smoothies can be a quick, delicious and nutritious way to fill in some of those food gaps during the day.

Breakfast is the biggest and most important challenge for most people. Smoothie meals are the ultrafast, simple answer. Even if you're constantly locked in a battle for time, it's easy to make a smoothie and sip it while you get ready in the morning. Or, blend it up and take it with you.

2. An Easy Way To Get More Fruits & Vegetables

If 5 to 9 servings of fruits and vegetables seems like some impossible mountain of produce, power smoothies will come to your rescue. Each smoothie in this book is guaranteed to give you several fruit or vegetable servings to your credit.

And if you've been searching for a way to start eating better, just remember that the best approach is a simple one. Start with a few simple changes, but don't put pressure on yourself to change everything. You could get really tough with yourself and stop-cold turkey-all those bad eating habits. But, in the long run, hardly anyone is successful with this approach. The pressure to be perfect becomes too overwhelming.

One easy way to begin chalking up more fruit and vegetable credit is to focus on breakfast. Even if you make no other changes at first, something as simple as starting the day with a nutritious power smoothie breakfast can begin to make a dent in those 5 to 9 servings that are so important.

The ingredients are simple to shop for and easy to have on hand. Power smoothies are so quick to fix and delicious, they're an easy way to take a big step toward a healthier lifestyle.

3. Power Smoothies Are The Perfect "Stealth Health" Vehicle.

Evelyn Tribole, M.S., R.D. says you can "eat right in spite of yourself" in her wonderful book, *Stealth Health, How*

To Sneak Nutrition Painlessly Into Your Diet. Although we called them "secret ingredients", we've used a version of the stealth health method for years. It all got started with carrots. One day we were in experimental mode whipping up a peach smoothie. We tentatively dropped some baby carrots into the peachy concoction. Voila! A peach carrot smoothie and you couldn't taste the carrot. After that we began popping carrots in lots of smoothies.

The point is, you can add some really nutritious items to smoothies that you might not necessarily eat by themselves. Carrots are just one example of a healthy food that blends in so thoroughly that you can fool yourself and not know it's in there. It's easy to get your 1-1/2 carrots a day (the official recommended daily carrot allowance per Dr. Ken Cooper of The Aerobics Institute in Dallas, Texas) using power smoothies. Try our *Stealth Nut Smoothie.* It may give you some ideas on ways to sneak healthy stuff in on yourself using smoothies.

4. "Drinking" Your Whole Foods May Be The Road To Maximum Nutrition

Recent studies have shown that some cancer fighting nutrients like beta-carotene (found in carrots, cantaloupe, apricots, etc) and lycopene (found in tomatoes, watermelon and pink grapefruit) are absorbed as much as 3 times more efficiently by your body when the foods are pureed versus eating them raw. Although beta-carotene and lycopene were the only food properties that were the subject of these studies, many experts believe that pureeing fruits and vegetables (as in a blender) causes many nutrients to be much more bioavailable (absorbed) by the body. Pureeing "breaks down certain chemical bonds in fruits and vegetables and releases the carotenoids" according to the July, 1999 issue of the UC Berkeley Wellness Letter, the premier health and wellness newsletter in the world.

Sure, you get enormous food value just eating a carrot. But you may just be maximizing the nutritional punch of that carrot by blending it up in a power smoothie.

5. Power Smoothies Can Help You Get The Snack Monkey Off Your Back.

I think almost everyone would agree that snacks account for, in large part, where many of us go wrong. Because, as snackers, Americans are world class. Believe it or not, we ate almost 11 million pounds of potato chips during last year's Super Bowl alone. Besides the chips, we average 4 donuts, a half gallon of ice cream, a half pound of candy, 7 soda pops and a couple pieces of cake per week. Whew! What a high calorie nutrition wasteland!

Snacks aren't bad in themselves. In fact, several studies have shown that breaking food intake into many small meals and snacks is more effective than the more traditional 3 large meals a day in maintaining a healthy weight. The key is to make sure that snacks don't contribute just to the calorie side of the ledger.

So, next time you're headed for the chips or the box of cookies, reach for the blender instead and make a nutrient dense power smoothie. Your waist and thighs will thank you.

6. With Power Smoothies You Can Eat More Soy Foods (and actually like them)

There's no doubt that soy has been making quite a name for itself. Soybeans are, by far, the best plant source of protein and the only vegetable food whose protein is complete. There is strong evidence that soy foods may help reduce both men's and women's risk of cancer, heart disease and osteoporosis. Not only that, regular soy intake has been linked to lower cholesterol and reduced symptoms of PMS and menopause. So, there's every reason in the world to make an effort to eat some soy foods every day.

If you're one of those people who have recently jumped on the soy bandwagon for the health benefits and then jumped off again because you were put off by the taste, or never really tried it at all, try our power smoothies made with our Ultimate Soy Protein Smoothie Mix. Our soy protein comes from a premium sweet soybean with a mild, nutty flavor. Whole Nectar Power Smoothies are a delicious way to get more healthy soy foods into your diet every day.

7. Power Smoothies Can Help You On Your Way Toward A More Balanced Vegetarian Diet.

Years ago, health people used to say, "If you're eating the typical American diet you don't need to worry about protein." This was probably a true statement at the time because most people in this country typically ate lots of meat, eggs and dairy products, all excellent sources of protein. Times have changed. Nutritionists have convinced us that these animal protein sources should be eaten sparingly and a more vegetarian diet is the way to go. The ranks of full and part-time vegetarians is growing. On top of that, many people have chosen to avoid dairy products even though the low-fat and non-fat versions are very healthful.

The upshot of all this is that if you've cut down on meat, eggs and dairy products, it's possible you're not getting enough protein. It's not that it's impossible to get enough from plant sources. You're just going to have to work a little harder to make sure you do. But it's still important that you do get enough, because protein has an important role in the human body - growing and repairing cells. How much protein you need is based on your weight and activity level. And while the experts sometimes argue the fine points of how much protein we should consume, no one suggests we avoid it. Just for the record - proteins aren't more important than carbohydrates or fat (as some of the fad diet gurus would have you believe) All three have equally important roles in human nutrition. It's called balance.

Our power smoothie recipes are a great way to help fill in any protein gap you might have if you're making more vegetarian choices.

8. You'll Get More Fiber With Power Smoothies.

The importance of fiber goes beyond it's ability to keep you regular. The fibrous portion of all plant food is loaded with nutrients. In addition, high fiber foods fill you up, break down slowly and help control your appetite. In spite of all the hoopla about the importance of a fiber rich diet, most of us aren't even getting half of the 20 to 35 grams recommended by the American Dietetic Association. The whole food, power smoothies featured in this book are inherently fiber rich and an easy way to get on track with a high fiber diet.

In addition, Barbara Rolls, Ph.D. believes that eating foods with low energy density (high water content and lots of fiber) are a key to achieving and maintaining a healthy weight. Her book *The Volumetrics Weight-Control Plan* is based on studies she conducted at Penn State University. Her work shows that those who fill up on "high volume" foods (like fruit rich smoothies) feel full on fewer calories and subsequently consume fewer calories overall without feeling hungry. Dr. Rolls maintains that a person who consumes 16 oz. of a low energy density meal (like a power smoothie at about 350 calories) feels just as full and satisfied as a person who consumes 16 oz. of a high energy density meal (like a burger, fries and a soft drink at about 900 calories). That 550 calorie difference translates over time into a significant loss or gain in body weight.

9. Power Smoothies Can Help Get You Out Of The Weak Meal Rut.
Our bodies were unquestionably designed to run primarily on nutrient dense foods like fruits, vegetables, nuts, seeds and whole grains. The design of our digestive system tells us that this is true. But the most commonly eaten foods in this country are white bread, hot dogs and pop. The fact that we're not all 400 pounds or dead by age 30 is a testimonial in itself to the tough and adaptable nature of the human body. Complaints like headaches, fatigue, overweight, constipation, ulcers, colds, flu, allergies and digestive problems are now at epidemic proportions. In fact, many experts believe that these low level, persistent complaints are warning signs of subclinical levels of malnutrition. And, what then are the consequences of a couple decades of poor eating? Cancer, heart disease and diabetes, to name a few.
While experts sort through the details, the big picture is already clear. The human body has an amazing ability to fight off the effects of stress, air pollution, pesticides and all kinds of toxic chemicals, but only if it's well nourished. A low fat diet, rich in fruits, vegetables and whole grains is not just important, it's vital to your quality of life at all times of your life.

If nutritious whole foods are not yet the focus of your eating plan, you can't afford to spend any more time in the weak meal rut, over-fueled with calories but under-nourished. Power smoothies can help you break free of a routine of nutritionally counterfeit food.

The Whole Nectar
Healthy Lifestyle Philosophy

Don't put off making healthy lifestyle changes
just because you can't be perfect.

No more excuses about not having enough time.
Don't wait to begin doing things you know are important
because you're hoping for more time to magically appear.
It won't.

Stop worrying about the never ending details,
and sometimes controversial elements, of a healthy
lifestyle. Even if you do nothing else right,
do these biggies every day:

1. Take some small steps toward smarter
   food choices.
2. Blend, drink and enjoy lots of delicious
   fruits, and vegetables.
3. Take a brisk walk, and laugh a lot.

The rest will fall into place.

Blender vs. Juicer
If you want all the health benefits,
which one should you choose?

We've all heard every health, wellness, fitness and diet expert on the planet recommend a whole food diet. Plain and simply stated - a diet rich in fruit and vegetables is a key to vibrant health. The experts may argue among themselves about certain fine points of nutrition. None of them would argue, however, that we would all be markedly better off if we ate more generously from the produce department.

More and more studies are showing that whole foods are complex, nutrient dense packages loaded with phytochemicals that work synergistically to keep us healthy.

So, how does your typical juice fit into the whole food eating philosophy? Tastes good. But what about all the fiber that got thrown away when the processing plant or the home juice extractor made the juice? Up to 70% of the nutrition in most fruits and vegetables (including lots of those antioxidants we all need so badly) are in the fibrous parts of plants. That makes grocery store or home extracted juice a nutritional shadow of it's former whole food self. So much so, that many registered dieticians like Judy Fitzgibbons, R.D.,a syndicated columnist for Tribune Media Services, believe that most juice shouldn't "count" at all toward the recommended 5 to 9 servings of fruits and vegetables.

Enter the blender. Blenders make juice by liquifying the whole food. Nothing is separated out or thrown away. In fact, the juice you make in a blender is really much more than juice - it's the nectar of the whole food.

Best of all, you can use your blender to take these whole food nectars one step farther and create some delicious, protein-balanced smoothies.

"Put your juicer in the attic and get a blender"

Advises Dr. Herbert Pierson, former project director of the National Cancer Institute's Cancer Preventative Designer Foods Project. "Most benefits are in the fiber and pulpy parts of fruit."

Key Nutrients / Phytochemicals In Power Smoothie Ingredients

Almond (calcium, Vit E, ellagic acid, beneficial fats)
Apple (fiber-pectin)
Apricot (Vit A, beta-carotene)
Banana (potassium)
Berry (anthocyanidins, ellagic acid, Vit C, potassium)
Cantaloupe (Vit A, beta-carotene, Vit C, potassium)
Carrot (Vit A, beta-carotene)
Cherry (Vit C)
Date (potassium)
Flax Seed (lignans)
Grape (resveratrol, ellagic acid)
Grapefruit (Vit C, flavanones)
Guava (Vit C, pectin)
Kiwi (Vit C)
Lemon (Vit C, flavanones)
Mango (Vit A, beta-carotene)
Melon (potassium, Vit C)
Nectarine (Vit C, A, beta-carotene)
Oat (fiber, protein, iron, manganese, saponins)
Orange (Vit C, flavanones)
Papaya (carotenoids)
Peach (Vit C, A)
Peanut Butter (protein, fiber, thiamin, niacin)
Pear (fiber, Vit C)
Pineapple (bromelain)
Soy Smoothie Mix (isoflavonoids, lignans, protein, calcium)
Sunflower Seeds (Vit E, B6, magnesium, zinc)
Yogurt (calcium, protein)

Phyto Primer

I'm sure you've seen the term "phytochemical" batted around both in the press and in this book. Phyto's are important, so here's a little rundown on what they are:

Phytochemicals are substances in all plant life that give plants their flavor, color, and smell. In addition, these plant chemicals protect the plant from disease, air pollution, radiation damage and can even act as insect repellent.

Perhaps the most amazing thing about phytos is that when you eat them, they protect you from disease, too. Phytochemicals have been getting an increasing amount of press as studies begin to show that they fight everything from cancer to wrinkles. (And if we're lucky, scientists will also figure out how phytos can act as insect repellent for people, too.) Over 4000 of these substances have been discovered so far and that may not even be the half of it. Of the 4000, only about 150 or so have really been studied.

One much publicized group of phytochemcials is the large family of flavonoids. As you might expect from the name, many are responsible for the flavor in food. For instance, the phytochemical allylic sulfide gives garlic it's distinctive taste.

Another large group of phytochemicals are the carotenoids. Many carotenoids are plant pigments such as beta-carotene that makes carrots orange.

Many phytochemicals appear to fight disease by acting as antioxidants - they defeat disease causing free radicals by balancing the chemistry of cells in ways we are only beginning to understand.

Scientists don't yet know what a lot of these substances do. What they do know is that most of them appear to work synergistically with each other and with vitamins, minerals, hormones, etc. The importance of this interaction has become readily apparent as a result of experiments that have been done using phytochemicals extracted out of their natural environment in food. Guess what. The extracts don't work nearly as well as the food itself. The protective affect of beta-carotene, for instance, appears to result from it's combined action with several other carotenoids that occur naturally in food.

The bottom line is "while vitamin and mineral supplements make sense in some cases, phytochemical supplements do not" according to the April, 1999 issue of the UC Berkeley Wellness Letter. To stay healthy, you need to eat the whole food with all of the phytochemicals in their natural ratios.

And there is no one super food. Eat a variety of fruits, vegetables and whole grains and you'll get all the phytos you need.

How To Pick The Best Fruit
& how to store it when you get home

Fruit	What To Look For	Storage
apples	smooth, unbruised, kept cold	refrigerate from picking to eating
apricots	plump, soft, perfumy	room temperature until ripe then plastic bag in refrigerator
banana	any stage of ripeness	room temperature
berries (except strawberry)	plump, firm, mold free	in shallow, wide bottom plastic container lined with paper towels in refrigerator
cherries	plump, firm, dark, even colored, with stem, kept cool	loosely packed in plastic bag in refrigerator
cranberries	plump, firm, uniformly colored	freeze in original bag from store
grapes	plump, firmly attached to to stem, kept cool, powdery bloom is sign of freshness	left on stem in plastic bag in refrigerator
grapefruit	round, flattened end, should should feel heavy for size	room temperature for a week and then refrigerate
guava	greenish yellow or yellow, fragrant	room temperature
kiwi	plump, fragrant, yield under pressure	room temperature for a couple of days until ripe (soft) then refrigerate in plastic bag

Fruit	What To Look For	Storage
lemons	bright yellow, glossy, firm but not hard, heavy fruit with fine grained skin has the most juice	room temperature for about a week then refrigerate
lime	bright green, glossy, firm but not hard, heavy fruit with fine grained skin has the most juice	refrigerate in plastic bag
mango	yellow-orange or red, yield to slight pressure	room temperature for a few days until ripe (soft) then plastic bag in refrigerator
melons (except watermelon)	will feel heavy for size. blossom end will feel tender when pressed perfumy smell	room temperature for a couple days will make them softer & juicier but not sweeter. then plastic bag in refrigerator
nectarine	deep yellow under red blush, fragrant, yield to gentle pressure	room temperature for a couple days until ripe then refrigerate
oranges	heavy for size, firm, color not a sign of ripeness or sweetness	room temperature for about a week then refrigerate
papaya	yellow-green to yellow (all green may not ripen)	room temperature until ripe (all yellow) then refrigerate in plastic bag
peach	yellow-orange or red blush, fragrant, no bruises, yield to pressure	room temperature for a few days until ripe then refrigerate

Fruit	What To Look For	Storage
pear	unbruised, well colored, will be quite hard because stores rarely have ripe fruit	room temperature until until ripe and soft then refrigerate. Do not store in plastic bags.
pineapple	firm, plump, no bruises or soft spots, heavy for size, fresh looking green leaves, Hawaiian much high quality than Central American	will get softer & juicier (but not sweeter) if stored at room temperature for a few days. then refrigerate in plastic bag.
plum	plump, good color, yield to pressure	will soften but not sweeten if left at room temperature for a few days. then refrigerate in plastic bag.
strawberry	plump, no bruises, bright color, sweet smell, caps fresh and green	same as berries
watermelon	waxy finish (not real shiny, not not dull) yellow underside rather than white, heavy for size. rich red color if cut.	if uncut, can be stored at cool room temper- for a couple days but better stored on ice or in refrigerator.

Yes, The Paper Bag Trick Does Work For Ripening Fruit

You can speed up the ripening process of apricots, bananas, kiwi, mango, nectarine, papaya, peach, pear, and plum by putting them in a loosely closed paper bag at room temperature. Kiwi and papaya need the company of other fruit (like a banana) in the paper bag for this to work. One to three days will usually do it. Don't forget to check them every day.

Tips For Taking The Mess Out Of Mangos

If you've ever bought a mango and then made a huge mess trying to peel it, you're not alone. Don't let that damaging experience discourage you from enjoying a very tasty and nutritious fruit. Here's the peeling secret:

Hold the mango in your hand and score the skin in four lengthwise sections with a knife. Pull the skin from one section like you would peel a banana. Use a knife to remove the flesh from around the pit on that section. Repeat pulling back the skin and using the knife to remove the flesh on each of the other 3 sections. This method will remove most of the fruit from around the pit. The only way to get the rest of the fruit off the pit is to eat it off, like you would a peach.

To Peel Or Not To Peel

Many people are becoming aware of the fact that the peels of many fruits and vegetables are actually very nutritious and should be going into them instead of the trash. The Vita-Mix is a wonderful tool to liquify the whole food, including the peel, right into your smoothie.

The catch is, not all peels should be used. Some are strong tasting, for instance, and some are just not meant to be eaten. So, for maximum nutrition and good taste, how do you know which ones to use and not to use?

Here's What You Need To Know
Here are some very basic peeling guidelines for the most common fruits and vegetables:

Fruit-
Use the peel: apples, peaches, apricots, nectarines, pears, plums

Don't use the peel: avocado, pineapple, banana, melon, kiwi, papaya, mango, guava

Skim off the outer zest and leave the white pith on all citrus fruit.

Vegetables-
Use the peel on most common vegetables
except: beets, cucumber, garlic, ginger, onions, sweet potatoes, yams, eggplant.

Whether you peel or not, wash all fruits and vegetables thoroughly before blending.

For A Better Life, Hang Out With Good People And Good Food

All the knowledge and good intentions in the world won't help you eat well if you don't set yourself up to succeed. With a minimum of planning and effort you can insulate yourself from the high fat, junk food world by surrounding yourself with the right stuff.

We've had a lot of first hand experience with healthy lifestyle change - both personally and through working closely with other people. We've learned a lot over the years (sometimes the hard way). We wanted to pass along some ideas and suggestions that have worked for us, and other people we know, to make shopping and healthful food preparation, more effortless, more economical and even fun. We hope there are some ideas in the mix that will make it easier for you to make tasty fruits, vegetables, whole grains, nuts, seeds, and lean proteins the focus of your eating plan.

If your current grocery shopping routine is a little haphazard, work toward planning and shopping in 3 day chunks of time. Shopping once a week is a worthy goal, but tough for many people to pull off.

Use your computer to generate a shopping list of core fruit & vegetable items that you want to remind yourself to buy often. Keep this list in a prominent place in the kitchen. Add to it daily instead of preparing it from scratch just as you're headed to the store.

At the store, stick to the 3 day plan. Except for things like apples, which will keep for awhile, buy amounts of perishables that you will logically use in 3 or 4 days.

Instead of buying large amounts of a few items of produce, buy small amounts and more variety. Variety is healthier and you won't get bored.

Know how to pick the best. See our chart on *How To Pick The Best Fruit* and you'll be the expert in about 5 minutes.

When buying fruits like bananas, peaches, mangos, etc. select fruit of varying degrees of ripeness if you have a choice. That way they won't all be ready to eat at the same time.

Don't forget to stock up on non-perishable smoothie making essentials like frozen and canned juice concentrate, bags of frozen fruit, canned and dried fruit, and Whole Nectar Ultimate Soy Protein Smoothie Mix.

Fruit grown in the good old USA (including Hawaii), purchased in season, is your best bet for consistent flavor, freshness and low cost. Perishable produce flown from the far corners of the earth is usually expensive and can't match the quality produced by American farmers.

Don't get in a rut. Change your produce selections around from week to week. Our bodies were designed to run on a variety of whole foods.

Use the "rainbow" approach to your fruit & vegetable selections. The more variety of color the better.

Don't wash fruit way ahead of when you'll use it. It'll

keep a lot longer if you handle it as little as possible and wash only when needed.

We strongly suggest you check out our fruit storage tips on the *How To Pick The Best Fruit* chart on the preceding pages. With this knowledge in hand you'll get a lot more flavor and mileage out of your purchases.

If you keep your apples in a bowl on the table and your oranges in the refrigerator, it may surprise you to know that it should be the other way around (if you want them to last and have great taste, that is). See the storage tips on our *How To Pick The Best Fruit* chart.

If you end up with more fresh fruit on hand than you will use in a couple days, wash and freeze some of it right away.

Frozen bananas are extremely handy and delicious in smoothies. To freeze bananas, select ripe but not over ripe fruit. Peel and put whole banana in a quality freezer bag in the freezer. Don't thaw out before using in smoothies.

You can speed up the ripening of many fruits like peaches and pears by using a paper bag. For more information see the *How To Pick The Best Fruit* section.

Products like Fridge Friend, Extra Life and Evert-Fresh Bags have been shown to extend the life of fruits and vegetables by neutralizing ethylene, a natural gas given off by ripening produce.

Quick Tips & Information From
The Smoothie Institute

Your fruits and vegetables are the most important items in your refrigerator. Don't let them get buried in the back or hidden away in bins. Re-arrange the shelves, if necessary, so that you'll see them every time you open the refrigerator door. Put the ripest (the fruit you want to use first) in the most prominent place.

When storing fruits and vegetables in the refrigerator, don't combine different kinds in the same bag. Some of them don't get along very well together and will spoil more rapidly than if by themselves.

Make a Fruit Salad Power Smoothie once or twice a week to use up odds and ends of fruit, yogurt, juice, etc.

Very ripe, even overripe fruit make great smoothies.

Extra smoothie can be frozen in ice cube trays. Smoothie cubes can be used instead of ice cubes in making other smoothies.

Ripe fresh fruit like strawberries, peaches or mangos can be pureed in the Vita-Mix and frozen in ice cube trays to create fruit cubes. When the fruit is frozen, pop the cubes into a freezer bag. Use the fruit cubes in smoothies.

Put small pieces of fruit leftover from smoothie making (like half a peach) in a bag in the freezer. Collect these odds and ends for a few days and then use them in a smoothie.

About Whole Nectar Ultimate Soy Protein Smoothie Mix

If there is such a thing as a superfood, soy may be it. Soybeans are by far the best plant source of protein and the only vegetable food whose protein is complete. In addition, there is strong evidence that soy foods may help reduce the risk of cancer, heart disease and osteoporosis for both men and women. Not only that, regular soy intake has been linked to lower cholesterol and reduced symptoms of PMS and menopause.

With the recent flood of soy products into the marketplace, we are proud of our high-quality, unique, soy-based smoothie formula. If you've tried soy protein powder and were put off by the taste, we think you'll love the naturally sweet and nutty flavor of our Ultimate Soy Protein Smoothie Mix.

What Makes Our Product Unique

Unlike other soy protein powders, our number one ingredient is the whole soy bean - all the nutrition, including all the naturally occurring isoflavones in their natural ratios. We don't process them all out and then add some back in later like other products do. Our product is not a soy supplement from a laboratory. It's a soy food from whole soybeans grown in our own Midwest.

Our number one ingredient isn't just any whole soy bean, it's the *Ultimate Bean*, a special breed of premium soybean that contains 90% less stachyose and raffinose, the two sugars many people have difficulty digesting. Our *Ultimate Bean* is naturally grown and not genetically modified.

We've added just a small amount of natural sweetening.
Unlike most soy protein powders that are loaded with sugar,
the flavor and sweetness in Whole Nectar Smoothies
comes from the fresh fruits and other foods you blend with
the smoothie mix. The low level of sweetening in our
product means that you can flavor and sweeten any
smoothie for your own particular tastes. We're proud to say
our mix was specifically designed as a protein base for
creating healthy, gourmet quality, fresh fruit smoothies in a
blender. Our product is not a medicinal tasting "just add
water and stir" instant powder mix.

In Addition -

We've added a balance of the finest soy protein
isolates available to give you a full mealsworth of
protein. And this protein also comes from non-
genetically modified soybeans.

Non-dairy, lactose free and low in fat.

High in protein and rich in calcium.

Our Smoothie Mix Has A Very Short Ingredient List -
And That's A Good Thing Because What's
Not In Our Smoothie Mix Is Also Important

Sugar, sugar and more sugar. Most soy protein powders
are loaded with it because their number one ingredient is
soy isolate. Soy isolate doesn't happen to be very tasty so
manufacturers try to hide the taste with sugar and lots of it.
In addition, most manufacturers of protein powder are

aiming for customers that expect to make instant beverages (mixing powder with water in a glass with a spoon). This type of product has to be really sweet if you're only mixing it with water.

In contrast, the number one ingredient in our soy protein is a high quality whole "sweet bean" that doesn't require a boat load of sugar. And we're not in the instant smoothie business. We think the extra 45 seconds it takes to whirl fresh fruit and smoothie mix in a blender, is well worth it.

We have not added vitamins, minerals, herbs and other supplements to our mix. We could add any of these to our formula and it wouldn't raise the price of our product. And, on the face of it, it might seem like a benefit to have these additions in a protein powder. But, think about it. When these additions are in the mix, whether you're a 7 year old or a 70 year old, you're receiving the same supplement "dose" in a glass when you make a smoothie.

We don't think this is a good idea. That's why calcium was our only addition to the formula. In addition, supplements really affect the taste of protein powder and not in a good way. That brings us back to the subject of sugar, which is what you have to add to cover up the taste of the supplements.

Other Smoothie Mix Factoids

Our smoothie mix is a very versatile product that also makes great soymilk. Don't miss the easy directions in the soymilk section of this book.

The smoothie mix and the soymilk you make from it can be used in cooking.

Everyone should have emergency food storage. The best emergency food storage supplies are nutritious foods that don't have to be refrigerated and are foods that you would use everyday, anyway. Our smoothie mix is an ideal protein source for just that purpose. Assuming you don't have a way to use a blender, you can make an emergency protein drink by putting 2 cups of canned or bottled fruit juice, 3-5 tablespoons of smoothie mix and ice (if you have it) in a container and shake well. It's not a gourmet smoothie but you'll be glad you have it.

To obtain additional copies
of this book, to order Whole Nectar®
Ultimate Soy Protein Smoothie Mix, or to get
information about other products:

Whole Nectar
31 N. 700 E., Suite 277
St. George, UT 84770
Toll Free Orderline: 877-863-2827
www.wholenectar.com

For more information about the
Vita-Mix machine and other products from the
Vita-Mix Corporation:

Vita-Mix Corporation
8615 Usher Rd.
Cleveland, OH 44138
U.S. and Canada: 800-848-2649
www.vitamix.com

Who Are The Smoothie People Who Wrote This Book?

Bob Mulligan, Ph.D. began promoting healthy lifestyles over 40 years ago and has always had a passion for great tasting food. Over the years he has taught in universities, developed corporate wellness programs, owned health clubs, appeared in national publications and on radio and television. Wendy Mulligan worked for many years as a corporate accountant for several major corporations, all the while moonlighting as a health writer and assisting Bob with wellness projects.

Together they live in the desert southwest where it's always a good day for golf and exploring the red rock canyons near their home. Their kitchen continues to be a hotbed of smoothie-making activity.

"It's traditional for an author to acknowledge individuals who made special contributions toward the completion of a book. In our case, the "thank you" has to go to the smoothies themselves - the subject of our book. We sipped them as we wrote and they energized us all the way through the project. Our special thanks goes to Banana Julep Shake, Mango Tangerine Smoothie, Blueberry Orange Smoothie and Vanilla Super Soymilk."

Bob and Wendy Mulligan